Identifying and Serving
Gifted **English Language Learners**

Equitable Programs and Services for ELLs in Gifted Education

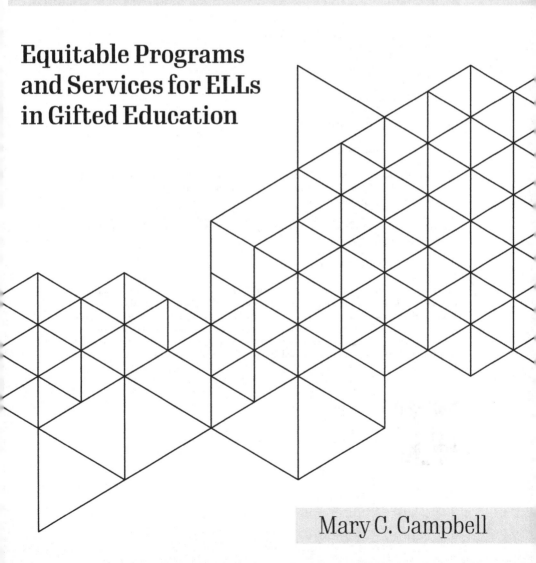

Mary C. Campbell

Library of Congress Control Number: 2020950492

Copyright ©2021, Prufrock Press Inc.

Edited by Stephanie McCauley

Cover and layout design by Shelby Charette

ISBN-13: 978-1-64632-060-8

Printed in the United States of America.

At the time of this book's publication, all facts and figures cited are the most current available. All telephone numbers, addresses, and website URLs are accurate and active. All publications, organizations, websites, and other resources exist as described in the book, and all have been verified. The authors and Prufrock Press Inc. make no warranty or guarantee concerning the information and materials given out by organizations or content found at websites, and we are not responsible for any changes that occur after this book's publication. If you find an error, please contact Prufrock Press Inc.

Prufrock Press Inc.
P.O. Box 8813
Waco, TX 76714-8813
Phone: (800) 998-2208
Fax: (800) 240-0333
http://www.prufrock.com

Table of Contents

Introduction
Who Are Gifted English Language Learners?

"Sometimes, being different feels a lot like being alone."
—Lindsey Stirling

"When everyone at school is speaking one language, and a lot of your classmates' parents also speak it, and you go home and see that your community is different—there is a sense of shame attached to that. It really takes growing up to treasure the specialness of being different."
—Sonia Sotomayor

I began my journey as an educator teaching English as a second language in a large, urban school district with a very heavy English language learner (ELL) population in the Southeast United States in 2011. During the first 8 years of my teaching journey, I taught all grade levels of students, including adult English language learners at the local community college. This book shares what I have learned about identifying and advocating for gifted ELLs.

Down the Rabbit Hole: Supporting Gifted ELLs

A short 6-year-old boy with a dark caramel complexion and molasses brown hair from El Salvador walks into his first school in the U.S. He is a smaller than the average first grader and has only been in the U.S. for a few days. In the preceding days, the boy met his father for the first time after being separated from him since birth, as well as the siblings that his father had while the boy was still in El Salvador. Today is his first day in a U.S. school. His classmates and teacher speak another language and seem to know so much.

The boy, whom I will refer to as Salz, grew more academically over the few months that I knew him than any of his other classmates. Salz ignited a spark in me that eventually led me to advocate for gifted English language learners. Advocating for gifted ELLs is something that I stumbled into, in a district that had just started talking about supporting gifted ELLs a year or two before.

To balance the opportunity gap between gifted learners and gifted ELLs, key players must come together to identify and support gifted ELLs. Traditionally, ELLs and students from racial and ethnic minority groups are underrepresented in gifted education, and most ELLs are overlooked (Aguirre, 2003; Castellano, 2003; Sanchez, 2017; Sparks & Harwin, 2017). According to an *Education Week* article (Sparks & Harwin, 2017), in West Virginia 1 in 100 students are English language learners. Of those ELLs, 1 in 100 may attend a school that offers a gifted education program. This means that only 0.0001% of those English language learners even have the opportunity to excel in a gifted academic program. Sanchez (2017) highlighted the inequities within Oklahoma to show that 10% of its students are identified as gifted, while only 2% of English language learners are identified as gifted. More shocking, states with higher populations of English language learners, such as California and Nevada, have an even wider identification gap between gifted students and gifted ELLs. There is an 18% gap in Nevada and a 19% gap in California between gifted students and gifted ELLs. Opportunities for gifted English language learners are rare, even after many have overcome the obstacles to enter U.S. schools (Gonzalez, 2016).

Sadly, cases like Salz's are not unique and happen at many schools across America every day. *Enrique's Journey: The Story of a Boy's Dangerous Odyssey to Reunite With His Mother* by Sonia Nazario (2006) highlights the many challenges that immigrants from Latin America face to enter the U.S. and rejoin their families. The heartbreaking story follows one boy as he tries and tries again to rejoin his family in the U.S. According to the U.S. Census Bureau (2017), Hispanics constitute 18.1% of the total U.S. population, while the total foreign-born population constitutes 13.7% percent of the total U.S. population. A large number of ELLs are born in the U.S., despite the common misconception that all ELLs were born in another country. Experience teaching ELLs informed me that many are born in the U.S., grow up in homes where English is not the first language, and enter U.S. schools with limited English. Data from the U.S. Department of Education (n.d.) show that in 2014–2015, 75% of ELLs were Hispanic or Latino, 11% were Asian, 6% were White, and the remaining were a varied mix of ethnicities. This leads to the questions: What is ESL? Who are ELLs? Who are ELL teachers?

The Who, What, When, Where, and Why of ESL

English as a second language (ESL) is a federally funded program to ensure that students who speak a language other than English as their first language receive instruction that (1) teaches English and (2) teaches academic content. All public schools in the U.S. are federally required to offer such programs as part of Public Law 107-110 from the No Child Left Behind Act (NCLB, 2001) and as a result of *Lau v. Nichols* (1974). The Every Student Succeeds Act (ESSA) bolstered the NCLB legislature in 2015 with added parameters that require states to track the academic progress of ELLs to ensure that they receive equal educational opportunities. These laws were created to ensure equally rigorous learning opportunities for English language learners across America who previously were disregarded in some states or taught using watered-down curriculum because of language barriers.

An ELL is any student in U.S. schools who is learning English as measured through that state's language proficiency parameters. The most common national and standardized language proficiency exam is the WIDA-ACCESS Placement Test (W-APT), an English entry exam to place possible ELLs, and an annual language assessment known as ACCESS measures language growth and proficiency. More than 40 states in the U.S. are considered WIDA states, meaning they use the W-APT to place ELLs and the ACCESS test to measure growth and English proficiency (WIDA, n.d.). Other notable states that are not WIDA states include New York, Arizona, and California. New York and California use an individualized interview process with questions for potential ELLs, while Arizona uses its own language proficiency assessment. The purpose of these assessments is to identify students who may need additional academic language support, and the process is typically initiated through a Home Language Survey (HLS) in which the parents or legal guardians indicate the most spoken language in the home, the most spoken language of the child, and if any other language may be spoken in the home. After the HLS is completed, students are then assessed to determine their eligibility for academic English support. If they fit the outlined criteria, as appropriate for their state's guidelines, then students are identified as ELLs until they are able to successfully demonstrate language proficiency through a state-outlined assessment.

An ELL or ESL teacher is a certified teacher who teaches ELLs how to listen, speak, read, and write in English. Certified ESL teachers have at least a bachelor's degree and possibly a master's degree, and have passed the state's necessary exam for English as a second language. They may hold multiple licensures, as needed, in different states, such as general education with a specialization in English learning, or they may only have an ESL licensure as approved by that state.

The Story of Salz

The journey for most ELLs typically begins with hardship and determination, as many pick up their whole lives and families to move to a new area for greater opportunities. This is especially true for Salz.

Salz joined my English learning group knowing little to no English besides "Hi" and "My name is." He always smiled at everyone and clearly wanted to make friends. I quickly learned that Salz did not know the letters of the alphabet, let alone how to read, but he always carried an interest in all of his surroundings. Whenever I looked at him, if he wasn't smiling back at me, he was clearly studying everyone and everything.

The first month that I knew him, he would mostly just smile and repeat or copy basic communication skills that his classmates or I would use. He could easily make friends in his classroom because he was always smiling, even though he couldn't have a conversation with fellow classmates. In the months following, Salz learned all of his letters and sounds, could read word families such as "cat, hat, bat, sat," and grew to read numerous sight words. He had made almost a year and half of growth in less than a semester. I became fascinated with Salz's academic growth, and so did his first-grade teacher. We both were surprised by Salz's academic drive, despite some of the many challenges he faced. After about a month of being at the school, he ended up moving in with his grandmother and had to take a taxi to and from school every day. He had little to no support at home, but he always managed to do his homework. He was driven and loved to learn. Over those months, he flourished academically with a smile the whole way. His teacher and I both recognized this spark in Salz and felt like he could benefit from some more challenging activities. But at this time in my teaching career, I did not know what that could include, nor did I know that much about gifted education. I had read a few books in college about gifted students but never received any formal or applicable information to use with gifted ELLs. This spark that I saw in Salz made me want to learn more about gifted education. I wanted to learn more about ways to support ELLs who need to be challenged academically. I wanted to learn more about gifted ELLs.

Despite this desire, I did not learn about ways to support gifted ELLs in time to reach Salz. He left after about 5 months of being at our school to go to another school or state, but his teacher and I never found out where he moved. We never heard from him again. He is one of many students I have taught over the years who ended their schooling with me abruptly and without any follow-up upon departure.

The following year, the academically or intellectually gifted (AIG) teacher at my school moved into the classroom right across from my own. Melanie Ragin, guru in the field of gifted education, became one of my closest coworkers over the next 5–6 years. She taught me about gifted education—what it looks like, sounds like, and how to foster opportunities for potentially gifted students to demonstrate their abilities. She guided me and the rest of our school in the creation of a culture of advocacy for any and all gifted students. This culture of advocacy centered on all of the staff being able to recognize and identify potentially gifted students. She also taught me about the indicators for gifted students and what gifted work could look like in different settings and subjects. Melanie became my partner in this work to identify more gifted ELLs throughout our school.

The Who, What, When, Where, and Why of Giftedness

Historically, the label of gifted indicates a belief in a person's ability to perform at a higher level than others (e.g., Coleman & Cross, 2005; Freehill, 1961; Hildreth, 1966). The tradition of identifying gifted students dates back as early as ancient Greece in the works of Plato noting his belief that there were children across all levels of society that held innate abilities to do better than others. These children were sought after and identified to receive separate education in the areas of philosophy and science (Freehill, 1961). In the 8th century, Emperor Charlemagne continued this belief by seeking to find the talent of the common man (Hildreth, 1966). In the 15th and 16th centuries, the Turkish Empire sought to recruit gifted children throughout the land to learn about Islamic arts, science, and history at a specialized school in Constantinople (Freehill, 1961; Hildreth 1966).

Then, in early American history, Thomas Jefferson advocated for the identification and special education of children with gifted abilities at the public's expense, later known as public education. Jefferson wrote, "We hope to avail the State of these talents which nature has sown as liberally among the poor as the rich, but which perish without use, if not sought for and activated" (Hildreth, 1966, p. 143). This belief in students with special talents and abilities led to the creation of many gifted programs across America in the mid-20th century, but these programs had limited guidelines and specifications required from the federal government. It also created room for numerous myths and misconceptions regarding gifted ELLs.

Due to the long history of gifted education and its many forms, there are numerous definitions and beliefs surrounding the identification of giftedness. Table 1 is a synthesis of the many definitions of giftedness (Coleman & Cross, 2005). For the purpose of this book, I will be using Marland's (1972) definition of gifted children from his report to Congress:

> Gifted and talented children are those identified by professional qualified people who, by virtue of outstanding abilities, are capable of high performance. These are children who require differentiated educational programs and/or services beyond those normally provided by the regular school program in order to realize their contribution to self and society.

According to the National Association for Gifted Children (NAGC, n.d.), there are numerous ways to assess or identify a child's giftedness, including observations, standardized assessments, academic or achievement measures, or student work samples using a standard measurement tool. One commonly used prescreener is the Gifted Rating Scales (GRS; Pfeiffer & Jarosewich, 2003), a Likert survey in which the classroom teacher rates every student compared to their same-age peers based on observations. The GRS uses qualitative and quantitative data to measure students' giftedness in the following domains: intellectual ability, academic ability, creativity, artistic talent, leadership ability, and motivation. The GRS may be used with students in grades 1–8.

Following the use of the GRS, districts may use assessments such as the Cognitive Abilities Test Full Battery Form, otherwise known as the CogAT, a group-administered assessment to measure students' ability using verbal, nonverbal, figurative, and quantitative methods. Other assess-

Table 1
Definitions of Giftedness (Coleman & Cross, 2005)

View of Giftedness	Definition
Achievement	Stresses general academic achievement and specific academic achievement.
Creativity	Proposes that creativity (i.e., the ability to do something new or novel in one's environment) distinguishes the truly gifted from those who are only very intelligent or high achievers.
Development	Supports the idea that precocity in a valued area indicates giftedness.
Ex Post Facto	Designates a person as gifted when they have made an outstanding and new contribution to society.
Interaction of Attributes	Conceptualizes giftedness as the interaction among various attributes.
Measurable IQ	Proposes that high ability in reasoning and judgment are essential to any idea of giftedness.
Omnibus	Sees giftedness as the demonstration of achievement, potential ability, or both in one or more specified areas.
Percentage Type	Proposes that a certain percentage of any group should be viewed as gifted or talented.
Social Talent	Recognizes the social forces involved in the development of abilities; proposes that giftedness is marked by consistent high performance in a socially valued activity.

ments include the Otis-Lennon School Ability Test, Henmon-Nelson Tests of Mental Ability, Raven's Progressive Matrices, and the Matrix Analogies Test. The Otis-Lennon School Ability Test also measures a student's ability using verbal, nonverbal, figurative, and quantitative questions. The Henmon-Nelson assessment measures students' intellectual ability and intelligence quotient, IQ. It consists of mostly verbal questioning with some numerical and figure analogy questions and is often criticized as having the greatest standard deviation for students who are exceptionally bright and those that possess average or below-average intelligence, as measured by its scale. This means that gifted students may not be identified using this particular assessment, as it relies heavily on verbal questioning instead of a more balanced and holistic approach to gifted thinking. Raven's Progressive Matrices and the Matrix Analogies Test are both group assessments for nonverbal reasoning. Both assessments are short in duration, taking only 10–20 minutes, compared to the CogAT and Henmon-Nelson, which may take multiple testing sessions lasting 45 minutes to a few hours each.

Additional assessments may be given based on student performance on previous gifted assessments, such as those listed, to assess student achievement within subject areas, such as reading or math. These follow-up assessments may include the Iowa Test of Basic Skills (ITBS), the SAT, and the Miller Analogies Test. The purpose of these additional assessments is to differentiate between students who may qualify as academically gifted, meaning gifted in a specific subject area, or intellectually gifted, meaning having an IQ that is above average.

Districts that are in the forefront of gifted identification allow students to be labeled as gifted in a single subject, gifted in multiple subjects, and/or intellectually gifted. These districts may offer a follow-up opportunity for gifted students to demonstrate their abilities using a student portfolio in which the AIG teacher presents a variety of assignments that may show students' gifted abilities, and students then choose a handful of activities to complete independently. Upon completion, the AIG teacher compiles the students' work samples and presents them to a team of AIG teachers to evaluate using set criteria, similar to the criteria measured on the CogAT. Affording students an additional opportunity to demonstrate other areas of giftedness, outside of a standardized test or one teacher's opinion, creates a wider net to identify a larger number of gifted students.

The advanced studies department in Charlotte-Mecklenburg Schools (CMS), NC, is a leader of change in the field of gifted identification, in large part due to Lisa Pagano, AIG and Talent Development District Lead Teacher. She is adamantly opposed to the misconception that gifted programs are elitist and has been working diligently since 2009 to improve the district's gifted program and increase access and opportunities for all students.

Some of the notable factors for the CMS (n.d.) gifted identification process include:

- All first-grade teachers are required to assess their students using the GRS.
- All second graders must be administered all parts of the CogAT (in a student's home language, if applicable).
- All students who score within a certain range within the CogAT must be administered the ITBS.
- A student portfolio assessment must be made available for any students meeting set criteria.

Pagano recognized a need for change in the process of identifying gifted students, particularly gifted English language learners. She worked with ELL teachers to modify and pilot a new identification program for ELLs, which added the following components (CMS, n.d.):

- a portfolio component (as mentioned previously);
- a talent development student profile, created by the current ELL teacher using the student's most recent language proficiency scores and the teacher's background knowledge of that student, to be used as data when considering and evaluating the student's work samples in their portfolio using language indicators; and
- the presence of an ELL teacher on the scoring teams measuring the student's portfolio work samples.

These modifications, implemented in partnership between the AIG department and the ELL department within the CMS school system, helped to increase the number of identified gifted ELLs. Although research of the plan's effectiveness is still ongoing and has not been published nor documented for public record, the number of identified gifted learners of diverse backgrounds has grown. Figure 1 shows the rise of identified students from underrepresented populations in the CMS gifted program, according to data from the Public Schools of North Carolina (n.d.). Although it does not clearly indicate the number of

Figure 1

Total Increase in Identified Gifted Learners From Underrepresented Backgrounds From 2015–2016 to 2017–2018 in Charlotte-Mecklenburg Schools (Public Schools of North Carolina, n.d.)

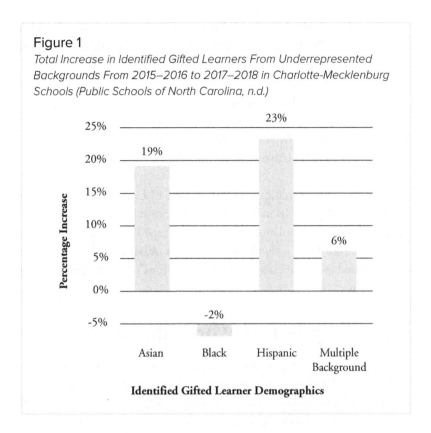

identified gifted ELLs, it can be inferred that some percentage of the demographics identified may include ELLs.

Who Are Gifted ELLs?

Gifted ELLs are learners who demonstrate above-average academic or intellectual ability in one of more various areas and who are learning English. They are students who are often perceived as having a deficit for not knowing English but are just as capable of being gifted as native speakers. According to Gonzalez (2016), more than half of ELLs in U.S. schools are born in the U.S. and live in homes where English is the second language. They may not be U.S. citizens yet, but they are legal residents in their home states.

According to the National Education Longitudinal Study (Resnick & Goodman, 1997), the representation of gifted ELLs broke down into the following demographics/ethnicities:

- 17.6% of all Asian students,
- 9% of all White students,
- 7.9% of all African American students,
- 6.7% of all Hispanic students, and
- 2.1% of all Native American students.

Unfortunately, findings show that gifted ELLs comprise only about 2% of the total population of ELLs, while research shows that approximately 10% of the population is gifted (Sanchez, 2017). Based on national data, there should be a significantly larger number of gifted ELLs who are identified and receiving academic extensions through differentiated curriculum.

Why Is This Work Important?

Before you can begin identifying and supporting ELLs, you must understand why this work is important. A colleague once told me that "gifted children are one of the most neglected groups in any school." It took me a moment to grasp what they meant because the critical thinking side of me started asking questions to contradict this statement: Don't gifted students have some of the most vocal parent support? Don't they already know most of the content? Don't they already have a wider knowledge and higher mastery rate than others? Aren't they some of the most cultured students?

Then I realized that I was rationalizing why some of the brightest students get ignored in classrooms across America and that my thinking was furthering misconceptions of gifted students. I also realized that almost every other group of students, including ELLs, students with Individualized Education Programs (IEPs) and 504 plans, students with learning disabilities, and those with physical learning needs, have clearly outlined legislation advocating for their educational rights, while gifted students have little to no educational rights. This led me to conclude that my colleague was correct. In the everyday classroom, these learners are quietly ignored while the teacher juggles the more pressing needs of other students.

Obviously, not all gifted students fall into the shy, quiet, passive learner category. Many are very vocal, active learners. These are the students who may be labeled a "smart aleck" or be sent out of class for arguing with the teacher. They may also be the same students who misbehave in class because they are bored from not being academically challenged. They, too, are often ignored because they already know or have mastered the content, and the teacher has to reach the ones who have not.

As you read the descriptions of both types of gifted students, you may have pictured a student you have taught—either a shy and passive learner or a more vocal and active student who may have been difficult to handle at times. Take a moment to think about students you thought may have been gifted. Now imagine the gifted students as being ELLs. Did your picture of the students change? Did the students you imagined morph into different students? Did your picture not change at all? Do you have any misconceptions of your own leading you to imagine one kind of student over another?

The National Center for Research on Gifted Education (NCRGE; Mun et al., 2016) conducted a literature review of six studies on the identification process of gifted ELLs. The data reflected that teachers may not consider ELLs as gifted due to (1) strong valuing of the English language as a characteristic of giftedness and (2) favoritism toward values that are important in American culture, such as individualism and verbal expression.

Imagine how gifted ELLs must feel in a U.S. school. Their teachers may hold misconceptions about them and assume they have a deficit because they can't speak English. Their teachers may choose to water down the curriculum because these students can't communicate yet. Maybe their teachers set the academic learning bar lower for them because they don't know enough English vocabulary yet. Maybe teachers only expect these students to memorize basic information, thereby only showing their level of understanding on the most basic level. Maybe these students have a unique and creative way to show their critical thinking or learning about a topic, but never have the opportunity to do so. Maybe they become bored with the memorization of topics and start misbehaving. Maybe they sit quietly all day and are never expected to talk because everyone assumes that they can't speak English. Maybe they start to believe everyone around them that they must be dumb because they can't speak English yet. Maybe they drop out of school, convinced that they are not smart enough.

Or maybe they enter a U.S. school with a teacher who believes they have an advantage because they can speak another language. Maybe that same teacher sets the bar as high or higher for them as for other students. Maybe they are given multiple ways to show their level of understanding. Maybe their teacher scaffolds the work so that they can still reach a higher level of mastery. Maybe they make friends and start to love school because people believe in them. Maybe they graduate with honors and go on to change the world. What type of educator are you in this scenario?

Only 2% of ELLs are identified as gifted, in stark contrast to the 10% of all students identified as gifted (Sanchez, 2017). So why is the percentage of identified gifted ELLs so much lower, and why is it so hard to identify gifted ELLs? This question has been researched and analyzed by NCRGE (Mun et al., 2016) with the following recommendations:

- ▶ educators need to acknowledge that giftedness exists in all populations regardless of race, ethnicity, and language;
- ▶ there needs to be a shift from deficit to strength-based thinking in the nomination, identification, and services of gifted ELLs;
- ▶ legislation needs to be created to mandate services for gifted learners;
- ▶ there needs to be more research in the area of gifted ELLs;
- ▶ states and districts need to acknowledge that standardized testing as a means of gifted identification is insufficient because of language and cultural bias; and
- ▶ states and districts need to use multiple measures and alternative assessments to collect a holistic picture of a student's ability.

Additional research found that states and districts need to analyze and develop a weighted scoring system to evaluate the multiple measures and alternative assessments (McBee et al., 2013). There also needs to be more professional development for school personnel, including teachers, for the topic of identification of culturally and linguistically diverse students so that educators may be knowledgeable about cultural characteristics of giftedness (Granada, 2002).

Measurable success in schools, districts, and states is evident where programs have been developed to increase the number of gifted ELLs. Fairfax County Public Schools successfully created and implemented a program to identify underrepresented gifted students, including those from low-income backgrounds, ELLs, and twice-exceptional learners. The program consisted of a multifaceted approach that included differentiated classroom services, direct instruction from the AIG teacher, and full-time programming with daily challenging instruction. This resulted in a 565% increase in the number of Black and Hispanic students receiving high school gifted services 11 years after implementation (Virginia Department of Education, 2017). Additional successful programs include Project GOTCHA (Galaxies of Thinking and Creative Heights of Achievement), Project CLUE, and Project IGNITE. Additional research from the U.S. Department of Education (Ross, 1993) acknowledges that gifted, creative, and talented young people exist in all cultural and economic groups. The data from these studies highlight the importance of this work to close the gap between gifted learners and gifted ELLs. However, it is not enough to know that this work is important; to improve and close the educational gap, steps must be taken by states and school districts.

Using This Book to Support Gifted ELLs

In order to address the underrepresentation of ELLs within gifted programs, key players—specifically school personnel, district leaders, and administrators—must be willing to commit to the process of using a multiple-measures approach (MMA) to identify potentially gifted ELLs. An MMA must be implemented in the nurturing, screening, identification, and servicing process of gifted program implementation. Additionally, school leaders must develop relationships with families and community members to facilitate a mind shift away from a deficit line of thinking regarding gifted ELLs and common misconceptions about who can and cannot be gifted. Moreover, potentially gifted students must be exposed to higher levels of thinking and creative opportunities, using instructional scaffolding and differentiated curriculum. Lastly, there must be ongoing training for teachers and parents to nurture potentially gifted students in kindergarten through fourth grade, as research shows these grade levels to be the most crucial in the identification process.

The purpose of this book is multifold, including to equip current ELL teachers with ways to identify and advocate for potentially gifted ELLs. It offers differentiation strategies for AIG teachers to use to illicit evidence of gifted abilities in ELLs along with supporting identified gifted ELLs. This book is also meant to inform and empower the parents of gifted ELLs with tools they can use to understand and advocate for their child. Lastly, this book aims to provide a clear methodology for districts and states to use to increase the number of identified gifted ELLs and to support them once they are identified. It presents the most notable research in the field of identifying and supporting gifted ELLs. It is also a practical guide for how to use these best practices at your school, or within your district or state. This book has been formatted into a tiered and sequential approach for each key player with a step-by-step breakdown explaining how to carry out each essential role in this process. Moreover, each chapter builds upon the content of the previous chapter or chapters to present the next steps in the process.

The five-part plan of action is as follows:

▶ **Chapter 1: Support.** This stage is broken into three key parts: (1) how to build an effective AIG/ELL collaboration team (what it looks like and signs of success), (2) how to establish a culture of advocacy and extend it throughout the school and greater community, and (3) how to build and foster parent relationships.

▶ **Chapter 2: Plan.** The next stage of this work is the planning process of considering how to nurture potentially gifted learners. This entails building upon the parent relationships from the Support stage to plan meaningful parent outreach events to educate ELL families. It also entails building upon a collaboration team and the culture of advocacy to effectively coplan lessons or units with the ELL and AIG teachers, as well as with classroom teachers. This step is an essential precursor for teachers to consider how gifted learners can demonstrate their talents.

▶ **Chapter 3: Listen.** This stage continues to build upon the system of support, culture of advocacy, and parent relationships to teach how educators and parents can listen and observe learners to look for indicators of giftedness. Educators explore the characteristics of giftedness, as well as what giftedness could look like in different settings and with different learning opportunities.

▶ **Chapter 4: Act.** This stage explores different methods for nurturing the observed gifts and talents to prepare gifted students for the identification process. It also examines some of the criteria used successfully by district and state programs to identify gifted learners from underrepresented populations.

▶ **Chapter 5: Teach.** The concluding stage of this process seeks to answer the question of what to do now that gifted ELLs are identified. It explores how to effectively support gifted ELLs using researched best practices, as well as next steps for teachers, support staff, administrators, and parents.

The rest of the book will explore each of these steps of action, along with the key players responsible during each step of the process. See Figure 2 for an outline of the Support, Plan, Listen, Act, Teach model.

This book is intended for the following key stakeholder groups:

▶ **ELL and AIG teachers:** Most of the work outlined in this book is dependent on a close collaboration between the English language, or English as a second/new language, teacher and the academically or intellectually gifted teacher in a school building. The close collaboration between these two teachers in a building is the starting point for this work. Both of these teachers must collaborate effectively and be knowledgeable about the other for this work to have the greatest impact. The sections within Chapter 1 offer guidance to develop this collaboration and to keep it growing all school year long.

▶ **Classroom teachers and other support staff:** Classroom teachers have the crucial role of identifying gifted potential using obser-

Figure 2
Support, Plan, Listen, Act, Teach

SUPPORT
- ▶ Create an ELL and AIG teacher collaboration team.
- ▶ Establish a culture of advocacy.
- ▶ Build parent relationships.

PLAN
- ▶ Plan meaningful parent outreach.
- ▶ Effectively plan to spark potential gifts and talents in ELLs with the ELL, AIG, and classroom teachers.

LISTEN
- ▶ Teach parents gifted indicators.
- ▶ Train ELL teachers and classroom teachers about gifted behaviors.

ACT
- ▶ Nurture potential gifts and talents in the classroom.
- ▶ Cast a wider net to identify potentially gifted ELLs.

TEACH
- ▶ Use best teaching practices for identified gifted ELLs.
- ▶ Share parent resources to provide ongoing support after identification.
- ▶ Meet the socioemotional needs of gifted ELLs.

vations, formative data, and academic measurements. However, this must not take place without the proper network of support; teachers must learn about indicators of giftedness and be supported to integrate higher order thinking and creative opportunities in the classroom.

- ▶ **School administrators and instructional coaches:** Identifying gifted ELLs works best when there is a strong commitment to the work by school leaders. Research studies on the effectiveness of gifted programs indicate that the success of gifted curricular programs directly correlates with the school leaders' commitment to the work (Iowa Department of Education, 2008). This work must be a schoolwide initiative that is supported and upheld by all school staff, especially school leaders (Iowa Department of Education, 2008).

- ▶ **District and state leaders:** As noted previously, the work of identifying underrepresented learners must be a collective effort that administrators work to implement. It must also be supported by district and state leaders, as they are entrusted with the role of determining curriculum and educational initiatives for schools to carry out. District and school leaders are encouraged to consider the data and research behind the multiple measure approach that casts a wider net for identifying gifted learners and to determine if this work is meaningful for their school populations.

- ▶ **Parents of gifted ELLs:** Parents of potentially or identified gifted ELLs must have support and become knowledgeable about what this work entails. They must understand what it means to have a gifted child, as well as how to best support them. The sections of this book that will be most beneficial to this group have a subheading that indicates that they are for parents. Parents are included in each stage or step of the process.

- ▶ **University-level future educators:** This book is intended to teach future educators about the importance and relevancy of identifying gifted learners from underrepresented populations. It aims to provide an extensive background on the process of, as well as the research behind, identifying and supporting gifted

ELLs to help educators make well-educated decisions upon their entry into the classroom.

The process of identifying potentially gifted ELLs cannot rest solely on the ELL teacher or the AIG teacher. It must be a collective effort, meaning that all invested parties must be willing to do what is in the best interest of children to carry out the various stages of this work. The following chapters provide this outline for invested parties, as well as guidance for how to carry out their roles.

Summary

Identifying gifted ELLs requires the knowledge of several key words and concepts that are the backbone to beginning this work, including gifted programming, defining ELLs, gifted testing, and the historical context of ELLs and gifted learning. Research indicates an urgent need for identifying and supporting gifted ELLs (e.g., Castellano, 2002; Kitano & Pedersen, 2002; M. S. Matthews & Castellano, 2014). Some districts and states are leading in the area of increasing the number of identified gifted ELLs, but there is a clear need for all districts to consider gifted programming changes to cast a wider net to identify these students.

Discussion Questions

1. Who are ELLs, and how are they identified in your community or school?
2. Who are gifted learners?
3. Who will be the key players for this work within your school or community?

CHAPTER 1

Support

Setting a Foundation to Support Gifted ELLs

"You can't build the plane as you are trying to fly it."

—Melanie Ragin, District Talent
Development Specialist

The most crucial part of reaching any goal is to make a plan. But before you can make a plan, you have to know your end goal. When Melanie Ragin and I began the work of supporting gifted ELLs, we didn't have a clear end goal or a long-range plan. We started working together and, over time, learned more about the other's areas of expertise. As we continued to learn about each other, we planned more and began making goals. Through trial and error, Melanie and I shared resources, planned lessons, and did different activities with our students. Over the years, we saw continued success with our students, particularly with students in grades K–2 because we fostered a culture to nurture possibly gifted learners. By my last year working with Melanie, we had become the first model site in our district for our work in collaboration to identify and support gifted English language learners. As a model site, classroom teachers, ELL teachers, and AIG teachers could visit to observe us teaching and explore our resources. We hosted panel discussions and offered guidance for other schools and districts to help them make similar achievements at their schools. By the end of my last year teaching in the classroom, we both felt proud of our work and commitment to gifted ELLs, and we are still good friends.

This is to say that it is hard to make a plan or goal without first building a strong team. In this chapter, you will learn how to build an AIG/ELL collaboration team, create a school culture of advocacy, and learn how to build parent relationships.

Setting the Stage for Effective Collaboration

"The single biggest problem in communication is the illusion that it has taken place."

—George Bernard Shaw

For ELL and AIG Teachers: Collaboration

The key to any good working relationship is communication. Not only is it useful in maintaining professionalism and getting day-to-day tasks completed efficiently, but it is also the backbone of the process of identifying gifted ELLs. This is especially true for ELL teachers and AIG teachers, as they receive little training about the other's field and rarely know what to look for to advocate for potentially gifted ELLs or to support identified gifted ELLs. For this reason, both teachers need to establish a strong working relationship to become knowledgeable about each other's field in order for (1) ELL teachers to advocate for possibly gifted ELLs and (2) gifted teachers to support certified gifted ELLs. Unfortunately, in many schools, ELL teachers are not advocating for gifted ELLs, and AIG teachers are not supporting identified gifted ELLs, not because they do not care, but because they do not know enough about each other, and therefore collaboration is not taking place. But that does not have to be the case. The following is an outline of how to start this collaboration process, signs of success, and guidance for you and your collaborating partner.

How to Start the ELL and AIG Collaboration Process. First and foremost, the AIG teacher and the ELL teacher should learn each other's names and where their rooms or offices are located. This may seem like an obvious first step, but over the years I have met countless teachers who have been working with the same AIG or ELL teacher and don't know their name or where their room is located. This can be a simple introduction that takes place at the beginning of the school year where you take the initiative to pop in and introduce yourself. As a part of this introduction, it is always a good thing to get to know each other a little better. Some good conversation starters may include sharing a bit about yourself, such as:

- where you are from,
- how long you've been teaching,
- if you've always been an AIG or ELL teacher, and
- anything personal you would like to share (e.g., family, children, favorite pastimes, etc.).

After brief introductions, get to know each other's schedules, including if their time is shared with another school or if they work part-time. By knowing each other's schedules, collaboration will be easier. You will also want to know when their planning and lunchtime periods are. Sometimes it is not possible to plan before or after school, so finding a shared time for planning during the workday may be the best option. A guiding document to support the early stages of this collaboration process is located in the Appendix B.

Next, get to know a bit about each other's caseload and the nuts and bolts of your jobs. This may include your busiest times of year, number of students served, and any big dates or testing windows. By knowing a bit more about caseloads and key dates, it will be easier to discuss planning times and key topics for planning.

At this point, you may want to go ahead and hash out your planning schedule. It is best to create a set planning schedule for the year so that you don't have to remember to send an email about scheduling planning time, and so that once the year gets going you both won't forget to plan. A good starting place for planning could be once a month with a set date, such as the first Tuesday of every month. That way, you both can add it this meeting to your schedule to avoid scheduling conflicts that may arise as the year takes off.

It is highly encouraged for the ELL and AIG teachers to have completed the guiding document "Setting the Stage for Effective AIG and ELL Collaboration" (see Appendix B) before the school year starts. However, the beginning of the school year is always busy, and some things have to take the back burner. With this in mind, teachers should meet to complete this form no later than the third week of school to be most effective.

Additionally, both the ELL teacher and the AIG teacher need to plan a date and time for the "Great Exchange," a meeting in which each teacher provides the other with a crash course of what they do. The Great Exchange can take place right after completing the previous guiding document, or it can be scheduled for a different time. The Great Exchange meeting is the crucial next step for both educators to be most effective in advocating for and supporting gifted ELLs. Appendix B also includes a guiding document to make the Great Exchange easier for ELL and AIG teachers, even if it is their first year in the role.

During the Great Exchange meeting, both the ELL and AIG teachers should share important key information about their roles and any relevant information or resources about their positions. The purpose of this meeting is to educate both teachers on how to advocate for, identify, and support potentially gifted ELLs. Therefore, each teacher needs to walk away with a strong foundational understanding of the other's role and processes. If, after this meeting, one or both teachers need additional support in their role with the process of advocating for, identifying, or supporting gifted ELLs, it is encouraged to have follow-up meetings to continue learning more about the other's position and resources.

How to Know You Are Collaborating Effectively. At this point, the ELL and AIG teachers have moved past the introductory stage, completed the Great Exchange meeting, and established a regular meeting schedule. But now what? What should these regular meetings look like? Ideally, both teachers will come prepared but with different resources.

The first meeting could establish norms for how you would like to conduct or carry out these meetings. Norms should include 3–5 key expectations that matter to you both and can be upheld for meetings to be productive, professional, and efficient. Some example norms may include: start and end on time, come prepared, keep the big picture in mind, bring solutions when presenting a problem, etc. Remember that these norms establish a positive professional learning community (PLC) or professional learning team (PLT) and should be geared to make these meetings easier, not add a layer of complication. So if you and your partner already have a strong PLC, you may not need to set up norms. Additional items to consider for this first meeting include answering/sharing:

- How many current gifted ELLs are identified in your school?
- How does that number compare to the past 2 years?
- What affected that number?
- What do you think are the next steps to increase that number?

After discussing and answering these questions, the ELL and AIG teachers should cocreate a SMART goal for the school year to identify more gifted ELLs in the school building. A SMART goal is one that is specific, measurable, achievable, relevant, and time-bound. As a part of this SMART goal, both teachers should explain their role in this process, with clearly defined checkpoints and expectations for those checkpoints. A possible SMART goal could be:

> This school year, 2021–2022, _____, the ELL teacher, and _____, the AIG teacher, will increase the overall number of identified gifted ELLs in our school by 5%, or three students, by the end of the school year. We will reach this goal by meeting monthly to discuss potentially gifted ELLs and how we can collaboratively nurture their giftedness so that they may be properly identified, either through the Gifted Rating Scale, portfolio process, or CogAT.

After creating a shared SMART goal, the ELL teacher and AIG teacher may want to break down what items may need to be discussed at different meetings throughout the year because of certain deadlines or testing windows. That way, both teachers will know exactly what to bring to each meeting and how they can prepare beforehand. To learn more about what these monthly meetings could look like, refer to Chapters 2 and 3 regarding planning and listening.

Signs of Successful Collaboration

For ELL and AIG Teachers. Most teachers I talk to about identifying gifted ELLs want a clear-cut model that they can replicate at their school or district. A teacher once asked me, "How do you plan what you teach and when?" I explained that I use multiple data points and then teach my students where they are, based on the data rather than on grade-level standards alone. I also explained how I scaffold and differentiate my lessons to reach students where they are and to teach them strategies to access grade-level texts, which I referred to as a happy balance. At this point, the teacher stopped listening. She responded, "Well, that won't work at my school because I have to teach what the classroom teachers are teaching." I realized that she had completely missed the point. Once she believed that she couldn't possibly support gifted ELLs because she has to teach to the standard, she gave up on the idea altogether. She thought that because she didn't have as much choice in what or how she taught, she couldn't possibly support gifted ELLs. Unfortunately, this line of thinking is not uncommon.

Success will look different from school to school, district to district, and state to state. Some schools have a push-in-only model for ESL or AIG. Some schools share multiple ELL and AIG teachers, so these educators may only be at a certain school for one day a week. Some ELL and AIG teachers get a lot of autonomy over what and how they teach. Others must only teach the standards in a coteaching model. The variations in these models and programs from school to school make it impossible to have a one-size-fits-all solution. Therefore, it is crucial to identify your school's model and consider what success will look like for you. The most obvious sign of success will be an increase in the percentage of identified gifted ELLs, but this will not happen overnight.

One of the greatest determining factors of the success of this work, after creating a collaboration team, is administration support. It is possible to do this work without administration support, but it works faster and better if you have the support. I have worked with numerous administrators at multiple schools and across districts. Over this time, I have learned that no administrator is exactly the same as another. I have also learned that data is the one common language that all administrators understand. Fortunately for Melanie and me, our data always showed that we knew what we were doing and how to grow students' abilities. This allowed us to have more autonomy over what we chose to do with our students. If you are an ELL or AIG teacher with limited autonomy, this work is still possible, especially with the support of your administrators. By including your administrator in this work, you gain another system of support for your team. You also gain insight into aspects of the entire school that you or your collaborating partner might have overlooked when creating your initial SMART goal. Some key questions to discuss with your administrator may include:

- ► What is your vision for identifying and supporting gifted learners at our school?
- ► How could you support us with this work?
- ► Do you think it would be beneficial for us to lead a training about this work with our staff?
- ► What additional information should we consider when planning this work?

Follow-up meetings throughout the year may include "pulse check-ins" in which collaboration team members share their progress toward your goal and plans for any parent outreach events or key information for staff. The purpose of the pulse check-in is to make sure everyone involved is on the same page, is equally knowledgeable about potentially gifted students, and can share any relevant information.

Once your administration team is on board with this work, you can start moving toward creating a culture of advocacy. If your administration team is not on board or is passively on board, you can still do this work; it might just take more time. To learn more about the next steps, see the next section, Creating a Culture of Advocacy.

For Administrators and District/State Leaders. For this work to be as successful as possible, you must be willing to support this process as needed in your building, district, or state. School system leaders within the 15 states chosen for Project GOTCHA concluded that there are four criteria that must be present for the program to succeed (Aguirre, 2003; Castellano, 2003):

1. ESL teachers who are also certified or knowledgeable about gifted characteristics and strategies,
2. administrators and staff who are trained in how to assist students in reaching their maximum potential,
3. a learning climate conducive for academic success, and
4. a collective belief that the myths surrounding students who are gifted ELLs are false.

Project GOTCHA, originally a program from Florida, demonstrated evidence of success in supporting ELLs using this criteria for 7 years in a row and then received additional funding to carry out these findings across 15 more states.

Support may look different from school to school, but the most important detail for administrative support is staying informed and making this work a priority for everyone in the school. As an administrator, it is not enough to just send an email or tell your school about this work; you must be willing to put effort and time into the work to get it started and keep it going.

One way to do this is by having your ELL and AIG teachers present professional development training about this work and how it pertains to classroom teachers. Another option is to host a book study using this text (see Appendix A). Additionally you could facilitate the creation of a larger PLC by extending the ELL and AIG collaboration team to incorporate one teacher from every grade level who would meet monthly as a PLC. Making this work a priority will send a message to staff members to help do their part.

As previously mentioned, this work is relevant in closing not only the gap between ELLs and gifted learners, but also the gap between ELLs' achievement and that of non-ELL peers. According to the U.S. Census Bureau (Ennis et al., 2011), Hispanics are the largest, fastest-growing, and youngest group in the U.S. They also have the greatest dropout rate when compared with other racial/ethnic groups (National Center for Education Statistics, 2010). The growing numbers of Hispanics in U.S. schools provides relevancy to the issue of identifying gifted ELLs to provide positive measurable results for districts and states that are committed to this work.

By providing more rigorous and highly engaging opportunities for all students, including ELLs, teachers will be able to spot potentially gifted learners and offer more critical thinking opportunities. This also can lead to more differentiation and scaffolding within general classroom lessons, and thus support a wider range of students' learning abilities.

For Parents of Gifted Children. The following is a list of ways that you can support your potentially or certified gifted learner to contribute to their academic achievement (Castellano, 2003):

▶ Discuss with your child the importance and value of achievement in school.

▶ Encourage your child to develop strong language skills and means of expression, both orally and in writing.

▶ Express your belief that your child will be successful through positive reinforcement statements, such as "You are capable of great things!" or "I believe you will do great!"

▶ Nurture a strong sense of family values, such as the importance of spending time together, helping each other with chores, and taking care of elders/younger siblings, and cultural values, such as the treatment of others or having pride in your family's history.

▶ Further this strong family connection to develop your child's self-confidence and emotional awareness to answer questions such as "Who am I?"

▶ Teach the value of hard work and persistence and how it can lead to success.

▶ Correct any misconceptions held by your child from others, such as deficit thinking, as an excuse for failure (e.g., "I am not good enough").

▸ Be involved in your child's learning and extracurricular activities to nurture your child's confidence and self-esteem.

Creating a Culture of Advocacy

"Unless someone like you cares a whole awful lot, nothing is going to get better. It's not."

—Dr. Seuss, *The Lorax*

According to NAGC (n.d.), gifted learners left unnoticed have been shown to develop anxiety, depression, and fears related to perfectionism and failure, along with higher high school and college dropout rates. That is why it is crucial to ensure that all classroom teachers are made aware of indicators of what giftedness could look like.

By educating all teachers and staff about indicators of gifted behaviors, as well as correcting myths and misconceptions regarding gifted learners, a belief is fostered that all potentially gifted learners can be successful. The wealth of knowledge is also shared for all parties involved so that they may become advocates for these students. More simply, if the classroom teacher and other support staff, including teachers who may work with students with an IEP or 504 plan, know about the indicators, they are able to advocate for students' special talents.

Common Myths and Misconceptions Surrounding Gifted ELLs

"The great enemy of the truth is very often not the lie, deliberate, contrived, and dishonest, but the myth, persistent, persuasive, and unrealistic."

—John F. Kennedy

To better understand the myths and misconceptions surrounding gifted ELLs, one must understand the historical background of immigrants, specifically attitudes toward immigrants, as America is often referred to as the melting pot of cultural identities. Anti-immigrant attitudes permeated the national atmosphere in the early 1920s due to an influx of immigrants following World War I. In the 1930s, resentment toward immigrants continued to worsen as studies reported that immigrants were genetically inferior (E. Diaz, 2002). Negative views of immigrants have fluctuated over the years and have influenced the educational system.

One of the greatest hurdles for the identification of gifted ELLs is the nomination process. It is one of the first steps in the gifted program identification process, but it is also the most subjective, based on teachers' preferences. In many states, teacher nominations remain the first step in the identification process, most likely due to the amount of time a teacher is able to observe and analyze students' potentially gifted abilities (Kitano & Pedersen, 2002). Research has shown improvements as well as a continued need for improvement (Kitano & Pedersen, 2002). These misconceptions must be corrected because in gifted programs teachers make the most nominations (McBee, 2006). Additionally, the teacher nomination process for gifted ELLs found that teachers' overvaluing of dominant cultural norms, such as verbal skills, social skills, achievement, and work ethic, drastically impacted the number of gifted ELLs identified (Mun et al., 2016).

For more gifted ELLs to be considered for nominations, educators and school systems must be made aware of these widespread myths and misconceptions that directly impact the nomination of gifted ELLs. The following list includes some of the most common myths surrounding gifted ELLs (Aguirre, 2003; Castellano, 2002; Kitano & Pedersen, 2002; Stambaugh & Chandler, 2012):

▸ Hispanic and linguistically diverse students are too shy or quiet to show leadership skills that most gifted programs are looking for in potentially gifted students.
▸ ELL cultures do not value the importance of school.
▸ ELLs can only be good in math and science.
▸ Gifted ELLs are almost always Asian.

- ▶ ELLs must exit LEP (limited English proficient) status before entering a gifted program.
- ▶ ELLs cannot be considered gifted if they are not on grade level.
- ▶ ELLs must be able to speak English proficiently to enter a gifted program.
- ▶ ELLs are less capable and unable to perform at the same level as other gifted learners.
- ▶ ELLs must acculturate to the dominant culture to understand aspects of giftedness.
- ▶ Parents of ELLs are not as involved as other parents.
- ▶ ELLs do better in groups and won't be able to do well working independently.
- ▶ ELLs have accents and limited vocabularies that make it too challenging for them to form their thoughts coherently.
- ▶ Culturally, linguistically, and ethnically diverse (CLED) students cannot be as intelligent as others—they may show their talents in different ways.
- ▶ CLED students have a deficit—they are poor or disadvantaged, so they can't succeed academically.
- ▶ Latino ethnic groups are from low-socioeconomic settings and don't have backgrounds in formal education.
- ▶ Only those who are White and middle class or higher can be gifted.
- ▶ Gifted children are not behavior children.
- ▶ CLED students should not receive modified curriculum; they "need to adjust to the majority culture in order to succeed" (Stambaugh & Chandler, 2012, p. 8).

Simply knowing these are myths and misconceptions is not enough. As an educator, you must become aware of your own misconceptions surrounding gifted ELLs. You must also realize that any student from any background has the potential to be gifted, and the action behind this realization starts with you.

How to Shift Away From Myths and Misconceptions

In order to shift away from these myths and misconceptions, you must recognize or become aware that each person holds biases and prejudice toward others. Initially, people develop these biases and prejudice as a means of quickly processing and sorting new information. They may draw an instant conclusion about someone based on the information presented to better understand what is taking place. For example, one may observe a community of non-native English speakers and draw a conclusion that non-native English speakers prefer to speak their own language. This conclusion is the brain's way of quickly processing an observation, much like what our ancestors had to do on a daily basis for survival. Our ancestors had to make snap judgments in life-or-death situations, which resulted in our ability to make similar quick judgments today. Drawing a conclusion and the conclusion itself are not in themselves ethically or morally wrong; it is how a person uses and refers to a conclusion that may cause challenges related to racism, sexism, bias, or discrimination. For example, if you used the previous example to assert that non-native English communities don't want to learn English, you would then be taking a seemingly harmless conclusion and applying it to make a negative judgment. In order to prevent these conclusions from forming into negative bias or judgments, you must retrain your brain to recognize that individual instances or beliefs do not represent "all" instances or beliefs. To do this, you must maintain an open mindset when referring to larger groups of people or cultures (Hammond, 2015).

Over the past 2 decades there has been a significant increase in the quantity of literature on culturally responsive teaching practices. A significant percent of that research examined how teachers' beliefs impact the academic mindset of culturally and linguistically diverse students. The following are three widely accepted examples of teacher actions that affect culturally and linguistically diverse students:

- ▸ **Microassaults:** The misuse of power and/or privilege to marginalize students of certain races or backgrounds, resulting in negative outcomes for CLED students. An example of a microassault in the classroom might be allowing White students to get away with inappropriate behaviors while punishing a CLED student for the same behavior. Another example would be excluding a CLED student from recess/outdoor time because they didn't finish their homework while allowing White students who didn't complete their class work to enjoy recess.

▸ **Microinsults:** The act of being insensitive or ignorant to the needs of CLED students. This may include teacher jokes about not being able to pronounce the names of students with non-Anglican names or ignoring special dietary needs of students when scheduling field trips. It can also include statements such as "They all look alike."

▸ **Microinvalidations:** The act of dismissing or invalidating concerns of racism or discrimination by CLED students. This can include a student bringing attention to an incident and the teacher playing down the severity of the incident by saying that the student is overreacting or being too sensitive to others. Other examples in the classroom may include statements such as "If you were nicer to others, then they wouldn't be mean to you," or "You always think people are being mean to you because you don't look like them." On a larger scale, these statements may include "If you don't want to be poor, then you just need to work harder," or "Most politicians are White men, but they succeeded because they were qualified for the position."

Mind Shift: From Deficit to Dynamic Thinking

To begin the crucial work of shifting away from myths, misconceptions, racism, and personal bias toward others, change must start on a personal level. This means pausing to recognize personal bias before taking action. One example might be thinking that Latino families care more about school parties than school curricular events and thus only sending families invitations to "fun" events. To correct this belief, you must first recognize the bias and then determine how to correct it. In this case, you could send home an interest survey for parents about the types of school events that are most important or interesting to them.

Additionally, teachers must properly address student concerns when they are brought to their attention, such as microassaults, microinsults, and microinvalidations. Do this by reminding students that they are not being overly sensitive, inferior, or irrational in these instances. Students should understand that their feelings are valid and that you will do whatever you can to correct the situation. Next, bolster students' self-confidence and self-assuredness of their cultural beliefs. This is when students transition away from feelings of inadequacy and self-consciousness toward positive feelings of "I am who I am, and I am perfect at being me." Start this process by celebrating what makes each student unique and getting to know their activities. As creatures of habit, humans gain comfort from feeling accepted in their (learning) environments.

The next step is to guide students to succeed in small, incremental achievements, such as solving a problem or completing a task. The process of guiding students to success builds students' self-confidence and self-esteem in their abilities, otherwise known as the "I think I can" mantra, which starts with the teacher. The teacher must express the belief that "Yes, you can do this because I know you can." This reaffirms the students' belief in their own abilities and reassures them that the teacher will be there to support them if they need it. Over time, the teacher will gradually phase out these reassurances because the students will have internalized their personal belief in themselves and, in turn, will no longer need as much cultural reinforcement.

As you move away from deficit thinking of ELLs, using the mind shift strategies, you can begin moving toward dynamic thinking. A dynamic mind shift focuses on the belief that ELLs are equally as capable of greatness as their peers and that ELLs hold an advantage by being bilingual, rather than a disadvantage for not knowing English completely yet. According to Lambert and Tucker (1979), one of the advantages of bilingualism is students' ability to transfer skills across languages. Vygotsky (2012) also noted that learning a second language helps individuals to better understand the structure and rules of their own language. Additionally, according to R. M. Diaz and Klingler (1991), bilinguals possess a greater metalinguistic awareness than monolinguals because they better understand language structures. Additional studies suggest that learning a new language positively influences higher order thinking skills, such as creative and critical thinking (E. Diaz, 2002). The process of recognizing the positive attributes that bilingual students possess helps educators to transition away from deficit thinking toward dynamic thinking of ELLs.

How and Where Does the Culture of Advocacy Begin?

Creating a culture of advocacy starts with you, whether you are classroom teacher, administrator, support staff, parent, nurse, psychologist, or all of the above. If you can't first advocate for those closest to you, you cannot move to a wider audience.

My culture of advocacy started with the ELLs in my K–2 grade levels, specifically the 5-, 6-, and 7-year-olds I taught every day. As I worked with them more and more, I learned little details about their lives, including reading habits and personal interests. I came to refer to this information as my Knowledge of Students (KOS), a phrase that I picked up in the pursuit of my National Boards. When I first came across the phrase, I assumed it simply referred to students' likes and dislikes, or knowing a bit about students' interests. I thought it was something that I, as an educator, had been doing the whole time, like learning what types of books my students wanted to read or what they wanted to be when they grew up. I quickly learned that this was a misconception when a mentor explained that KOS means knowing so much more about your students; KOS is an ever-evolving helix of knowledge, one that never ends and is constantly developing. It may include a student's likes and dislikes, interests, family background, learning journey, student data, and many more things. But most importantly, it is not concrete or finite. As adults, our interests are constantly changing and adapting as we see, hear, taste, feel, and smell new things—and that is after years of having many experiences. A child, even a well-cultured child, is still constantly evolving by learning and exploring new topics and content. They may go through a handful of best friends in one year, or they might learn about something that becomes their new favorite hobby. Therefore, as educators, we must also be adapting our knowledge of our students as we constantly learn new information about them.

Sadly, however, I have learned that most teachers who think they know their students actually do not. Once, at a training that I was leading for colleagues about building relationships with students, a teacher explained that she builds strong relationships with her students because she tells them "good morning." I thought this was a strange remark to make in a training about building relationships. It made think of this comparison: How many adults feel like the grocery store clerk really knows them because they say hi and ask, "How are you doing?" I think most people would agree that the clerk does not truly know anything about them from just those two remarks. So why would a teacher feel like just welcoming her students in the morning meant that she truly knew them? This remark made me realize that there must be some confusion about what it means to know one's students.

I realized that teachers needed more concrete directions for how to build relationships with their students. A second-grade teacher once asked me how to build a relationship with a new student who didn't speak, or couldn't speak, enough English yet to communicate. I chose to focus on a time in the teacher's day that centered around building student relationships: the morning meeting time. I observed the morning meeting a few times over the course of a week and noticed that during the share time, when each student shared their response to the day's get-to-know-you question, something odd would happen when it was the new student's turn to talk. Instead of letting the newcomer try to say his answer, the other students would tell me, "He can't speak English," and then they would skip the student. The teacher observed this behavior and thought it best to let the newcomer listen and hear others' responses but not answer. After my third visit observing the same behavior, I spoke with the teacher about her thought process. I suggested translating the day's question into the newcomer's language and then having the student draw or show his response. I also suggested letting the newcomer practice his share with a partner before the morning meeting so he would feel comfortable in sharing. The following week, when I returned for the morning meeting, the student was now sharing his thoughts, and the teacher celebrated that she had learned about the newcomer's favorite food, sports, and candy.

On another occasion, a new teacher asked me how to build relationships with students at the beginning of the year when there was so much to get done. I thought about sharing my list of get-to-know-you and student questionnaire activities, like glyphs and drawings, but I chose to share one of my favorite and easiest relationship-building strategies: listening. I explained to the teacher that she would be amazed at what her students were itching to share with her. So how do you truly listen to students? I do it by allocating specific share time at the beginning of every week and after any extended break from school. I make it clear to all students that everyone will have a chance to share, if they want to, and that we will all show respect and understanding toward the speaker. I then let students take turns sharing in a circle format in which, after each share, the class responds to the person who shared. Because most of my students are 5, 6, and 7, most of the responses are a lot of "me too," as students share about going to the park or seeing the newest Marvel movie, but they are able to see that the class cares about each other and one another's interests. I also make it a point to remember what students share and follow up with them about important events in their lives. For example, I had a student whose team had made it into a soccer championship, but I was unable to make the game. However, the next day I saw the student, I made sure to ask about his favorite part of the game. This made him happy even though his team didn't win the tournament because he knew that I cared about him.

I also guided the new teacher to consider how to truly listen to students with culturally and linguistically diverse backgrounds. The following are four ways to not only hear students, but also truly listen to them:

▶ Give the speaker your full attention to absorb what is being said.

▶ Consider the feelings that the speaker is trying to convey and be considerate to the emotions being expressed.

▶ Abate judgment and empathize with the subject.

▶ Recognize and respect cultural variations in communication (Hammond, 2015, p. 78).

To further develop a foundation of trust between yourself and students, seek opportunities to share your personal background and interests, as well as your concern and knowledge for issues that are important to students. By showing students that you were and are vulnerable, you humanize yourself in their eyes, making them see that everyone struggles at some point. In another instance, you may make it a point to show an interest in a student's life outside of school, showing that you are otherwise concerned with them as a person, rather than only in an academic setting. You can also develop trust with students by effectively teaching a concept in multiple ways. This shows students that you are able to meet them where they are and consider their personal learning style, rather than using only one teaching method that may not meet their learning needs.

Build Student Relationships and Your KOS

The following are activities that educators can use to get to know more about their students. An additional student interest survey is located on this book's online resources page at https://www.prufrock. com/Identifying-and-Supporting-Gifted-English-Language-Learners-Resources.aspx. The interest survey can be used with students in grades K–12. For students in grades K–2, administer the interest survey either one-on-one or through a whole- or small-group read aloud.

True For You Game. In this activity, give every student a sticky note, but don't take one yourself. Then, have your students stand and form a circle around you so that you are now in the center of the circle. Next, have students place their sticky notes on the floor where they are standing. Explain that for this game they will be moving around the circle to spots where there is a sticky note. They cannot move to the note directly on either side of them, and they can't go directly back to the note that they left. Then explain the concept of the game. To play, one person starts in the middle of the circle (preferably, you the teacher) and says something that is true for them, such as "I like the beach." If this statement is true for anyone else, they must step off of their sticky note and then find a new one to stand on. If there aren't any sticky notes left to stand on, they are the new person in the middle and must say something that is true for them. The class keeps playing until everyone has learned a little bit about each other. I usually ask everyone to share what they learned about each person before we end, to make sure we are all getting to know one another.

Balloon Toss. For this activity you will need one inflated balloon. Have students stand in a circle. One person stands in the middle holding the balloon, while everyone else stands around them. The person standing in the middle with the balloon says their name and one fact about themselves before tossing the balloon up and stepping out of the middle. Then another person steps in to catch the balloon before it falls. Whoever catches it has to say the name and the fact of the person before them, before stating their own. You can go in any order, and whoever wants to go next can go. This takes some of the pressure off of people who may be more shy. The best part is that other people in the group can help whoever catches the balloon in case they need help remembering. Here is an example: Carly tosses the balloon up and says, "My name is Carly, and I like chocolate." Then the next person jumps in to catch the balloon and says "Her name is Carly, and she likes chocolate. My name is Kou, and I like video games." Kou tosses the balloon up, and the next person catches. They say, "Her name is Carly, and she likes chocolate. His name is Kou, and he likes video games. My name is Tao, and I like eating." The game ends once everyone has caught the balloon. Restart the game if the balloon falls on the floor before someone catches it.

Twister Walk. For this activity you will need a Twister mat, a drawing of the Twister mat on a sheet of paper, and a writing utensil. On the drawing of the Twister mat, use the writing utensil to make a map. Your map must start at one end of the mat and show how someone could get to the other side by only going forward or side-to-side. The map can never "skip" or jump over a circle, nor can it go backward. Make sure to keep your map a secret.

Now, have your students group together on one side of the Twister mat. Explain that the goal is to get everyone from one side of the mat to the other side without talking. Explain that you will not tell them when it is their turn, and that they must be problem solvers to figure out who will go and when.

Then, begin the activity. As students step on a circle on the mat, if they are correct, do not say anything and let them keep moving. Once they step on a circle on the mat that is not correct or part of the path to get to the other side, make a buzzer noise to let them know they made a mistake. When someone makes a mistake, they must leave the board for someone else to try. As students watch others, they should begin to figure out parts of the correct path and get farther and farther. Classmates may start pointing or showing the person walking which circles are part of the path, but they must still be silent. Eventually, a student will make it to the other side and can show or point for the others. This will continue until the whole class makes it to the other side. Upon completion, I usually ask students the following questions to guide reflection:

- ▸ How did you feel when you made a mistake?
- ▸ How did you feel when your classmates helped you by showing you where to go?
- ▸ How did you feel when you made it to the other side?
- ▸ How did this activity make our class become problem solvers?
- ▸ What lesson could you learn from this activity about persistence, or the importance of trying again and again?

Student Glyphs. A glyph is a visual or drawing based on the artist's choices or responses to the topics provided. For example, a student may complete a glyph of a pumpkin by answering different prompts, such as "Draw triangle eyes if you have brothers, draw square eyes if you have sisters, draw circle eyes if you have brothers and sisters, or draw heart eyes if you have no siblings." The student then draws the correct eyes on their pumpkin based on their response. Glyphs are a quick and easy activity for students to share about themselves in a fun, creative, and nonthreatening way. At the beginning of the school year, I always have my students create a glyph to share a bit about themselves, and usually my student glyphs match my classroom theme for the year. I have done star glyphs, apple glyphs, cupcake glyphs, and even little geometric monster glyphs. Figure 3 is an example of one of my cupcake glyphs. You can create or find any glyph that you think would be most fitting for your students to complete. You may need construction paper, scissors, and glue, depending on the type of glyph you choose to use.

I Like to Move It Activity. Divide your room into two halves. You don't need to move any furniture; just explain that one side of the room will represent one topic, and the other side will represent another

Figure 3
Student Glyph Example

topic. Then, as you stand in the middle of the room, ask a question with two answer choices, such as "Do you like the beach or the mountains?" Then say the question again, but this time point to the side of the room that represents beach and the side that represents mountains.

After they move, choose 1–2 students to share why they like the beach or the mountains. Make sure to explain that this is a learning game for all participants to get to know one another, and they will be expected to share what they learned about their classmates at the end.

All About Me Gingerbread Activity. For this activity, use the Gingerbread Activity sheet located in the online resources for this book (https://www.prufrock.com/Identifying-and-Supporting-Gifted-Eng lish-Language-Learners-Resources.aspx). You may want to create a teacher exemplar. Then, distribute the sheet and explain that students are going to create a drawing of themselves on their gingerbread cutout. I usually tell my ELLs to create a drawing to show the traditional colors and clothing of their culture or country. When they are finished, have all of the students present their drawings and share what makes them unique. This is a great activity for students who may feel embarrassed or ashamed of their culture, as this is a positive means to showcase their cultural heritage. Some of my students give their gingerbread person friends, family members, or cultural pieces that are significant to them. Figure 4 shows two examples of student cutouts with flags and traditional clothing done by first graders.

Circle Share Activity. This is a name and memory game to play with students in the first few days of school for everyone to get to know one another. It is crucial that not only you, the teacher, know everyone's names, but also the students know each other's names to create a sense of belonging among all of the students. To play the game, you and your students should sit in a circle on the floor and then begin sharing in a clockwise direction. To do this, explain how the share will take place: Each person will say their name, and the person who goes next will have to say, "I am _____ and they are _____". Each time a new student shares, they must reintroduce the individuals who have already introduced themselves, meaning that whoever goes last will be responsible for reintroducing everyone else. Talk about pressure.

I Can Do This. What About You? Students will stand or sit in a circle facing each other. The teacher or the class will choose who will start the activity, and then the person to their left will go next, and so on, until everyone has had a chance to share. The person whose turn it is will stand up or step into the middle of the circle to say, "I can do this

Figure 4
All About Me Gingerbread Activity Examples

. . ." before performing an action, such as a dance, a twist, or something that is uniquely them, followed by asking, "What about you?" The next person will stand up or step into the middle of the circle for their turn to say, "I can do this. . . . What about you?" Each individual will have a turn to share what they can do. You can either have the students repeat what their peers did before saying their own, or each student can just share what they can do.

Getting to Know You Web Activity. For this activity, you will need a ball of yarn. You and the students will stand in a circle facing each other. Start by holding the ball of yarn and sharing something that you have in common with someone else in the room. It can be that you both have sisters or like the same type of chips, or that you have the same shoes or speak the same language. Afterward, you will hold onto the end of the ball of yarn and pass the ball to someone else in the circle, but not the person next to you on either side. The next person will also share something they have in common with someone else and hold onto the string of yarn while passing the ball of yarn to someone else. Students will keep passing and sharing until everyone holds a piece of yarn and collectively you have created a web. Before ending the activity, guide students to reflect on why this activity is important and how being interconnected means you are all on this learning journey together.

Modeling Clay. For this activity, you will need modeling clay for every student. After distributing a golf- or tennis-sized ball of modeling clay to each student, present the task. Students will use the modeling clay to create a sculpture or 3-D model. Their model or sculpture should be a response to the prompt, "Define yourself." Students may make a representation of themselves physically or their interests, culture, or beliefs. Some students may choose to make an object that is a metaphor for themselves, such as a suitcase if they feel that they don't belong anywhere, or a representation of their family. It will take students some time to come up with their ideas and to then create them. Afterward, make sure every student has an opportunity to share/present their product that defines them. For time management, you may want to break this activity up over multiple days, such as Day 1 for brainstorming, Day 2 for creating, and Day 3 for presentations. It is also important that speakers feel accepted and valued for their product, so I usually refer my students to our good listening skills chart, and we all clap after each student shares. Sometimes, my students do "Wows and Wonders" based on presentations, saying something they liked about their model and/or asking a question about it.

Circle Share. This activity is very similar to the Morning Meeting, in that all of the students sit in a circle on the floor and then take turns sharing. I do this by having the person on my left share first and then the person to their left shares, next, and so on. After I teach this concept, I do not say anything in between students because I want them to get comfortable running the class discussion. I do, however, make it very clear that I am listening and care about their responses to the day's question. Some common shares include favorites, like favorite candy, favorite fruit, favorite season, favorite food, favorite book, favorite holiday, etc.

Trivia Insight of the Day. These are questions that you can pose for creative or critical thinking based on the day of the week. You can post these questions on your slideshow for the day or on the whiteboard. They can be integrated into your morning meeting or can be an extension for students who finish work early. Some of the questions/themes can include:

▸ Marvelous Monday: Who is the best Marvel superhero? Why?
▸ Travel Tuesday: If you could travel anywhere in the world, where would you go, and why?
▸ Wishful Wednesday: If you could have any wish, what would you wish for, and why?
▸ Thirsty Thursday: What is your favorite drink that you could not live without?
▸ Frozen Friday: What is the best thing to do in cold weather?

You in a Box/Bag. Every student will need a box (cereal, tissue, shoe, etc.) or a brown paper bag. Explain that students must collect at least five items to put inside of their box that represent themselves. These can include a piece of clothing, a flag, photographs, drawings, figurines, or anything that is meaningful for them. This activity may also take place over multiple days so that students have enough time to create a product that proudly represents who they are.

The activities shared in this section for getting to know your students are a great place to start your knowledge of your students. However, this list is not all-inclusive, nor is it simply enough to do a few of these activities. In order to advocate for your students, you have to truly know them. I used to tell coworkers that you truly know your students when you can paint a well-rounded picture with key details about every single one of them. For me, this included talking about where they are from, what their family is like, what they like to read, their learning process, who they like to play with, what they want to be when they grow up, their driving force for learning, their learning kryptonite or what holds them back from learning, and their greater aspirations, to name a few. This list must always be growing and changing, as children's self-awareness and interests change over time. This is why it must be a continual process, not just one that happens in August and September.

Extending the Culture of Advocacy

As important as it is to develop your culture of advocacy within your classroom, it is equally important to extend that culture throughout the school, students' homes, and the greater community.

One way to think about extending the culture of advocacy is through an analogy of a pizza slice (see Figure 5). For this analogy, the culture of advocacy fostered and nurtured by classroom teachers is the pizza dough; it is the basis of the entire pizza, and without it, the sauce, toppings, and cheese would just melt into a pile of goop in the bottom of your oven. If the work of the classroom teacher is the dough in this instance, then the addition of the support staff is the pizza sauce. Without sauce, the pizza would just be bread. Support staff are the extra layer of individual support for learners with varied needs. The next layer of this pizza slice is the cheese, represented by parents' involvement and support in their child's learning. Parents and families are the crucial element that defines this slice of pizza, and they are the key players that spend the majority of the time with their students and can foster gifts and talents. The last and final layer of this pizza slice is the greater community, or in this analogy, the meat and vegetable toppings. A student's greater community offers extracurricular and enrichment opportunities outside of a school setting, such as clubs, organizations, hobbies, sports, and travel. The community can also vary from area to area and culture to culture, much like personal taste in pizza toppings. The next section, along with the next few chapters, will explore how school support

Figure 5
The Analogy of the Pizza Slice

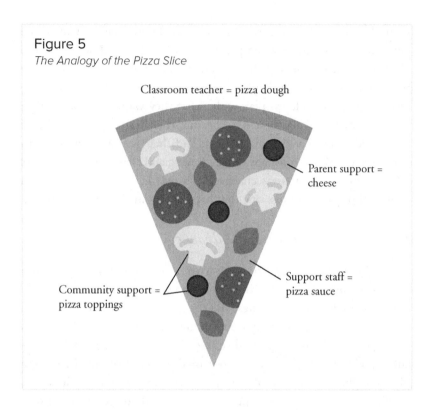

Classroom teacher = pizza dough

Parent support = cheese

Support staff = pizza sauce

Community support = pizza toppings

staff, student families, and the community can collaborate effectively to extend this culture of student advocacy.

Support staff in a school can include teachers of students with IEPs, the ESL and AIG teachers, as well as intervention teachers, guidance counselors, reading coaches, school facilitators, the speech pathologist, and the school psychologist. In addition to my close collaboration with my AIG teacher over the years, I also collaborated with our special education teachers, or teachers of students with learning disabilities or IEPs. This collaboration started out of necessity because I had several ELLs who had been dually identified as either ELL and AIG, or ELLs having an IEP. The collaboration between our three departments—ELL, AIG, and IEP—created its own culture of advocacy, as we collectively sought to create the best educational plan for students. Moreover, the culture of advocacy established among support staff added another layer of depth and meaning to the culture of advocacy being nurtured in the classroom.

The process of extending this culture of advocacy throughout the school, to encompass classroom teachers, support staff, and administrators, is the next step in this process after establishing a strong foundation of communication and collaboration between ELL and AIG teams. It is rooted in communication, receptivity, planning, and open, ongoing discourse between all key players throughout the school. It also takes time and shared effort to maintain. If not done already, this would be an ideal time for the ELL and AIG teachers to extend their collaboration team to include classroom teachers and/or grade-level representatives. If you do not have administrator support or classroom teacher buy-in, the process will still work, but it will take longer. You, the ELL and/or AIG teacher, will reach out to classroom teachers to discuss some students. When you reach out to classroom teachers, you may want to ask for a time when you could meet with them; it might be easier to discuss some possible students in the morning as students are entering the school or even during lunch. As you meet with classroom teachers, make sure that they have a strong understanding of what giftedness could look like, as well as ideas for potentially gifted students in their classrooms. This check-in with classroom teachers should also not be your first communication, as you will have already established a positive working relationship. Do not approach a classroom teacher with lots of questions (or for an information dump) during your first interaction, as this may send the wrong impression or create a strenuous situation for the future. In order for classroom teachers to understand what giftedness could look like, the AIG teacher may want to provide some background information. Figure 6 provides a framework for establishing a culture of advocacy among school staff.

Table 2 provides a detailed explanation of what each step entails and how to carry out that step. This table show key players (classroom teachers, support staff, and administrators) how to foster this culture of advocacy in incremental steps. By fostering a schoolwide culture of advocacy, every staff member is responsible for identifying and supporting potentially gifted learners.

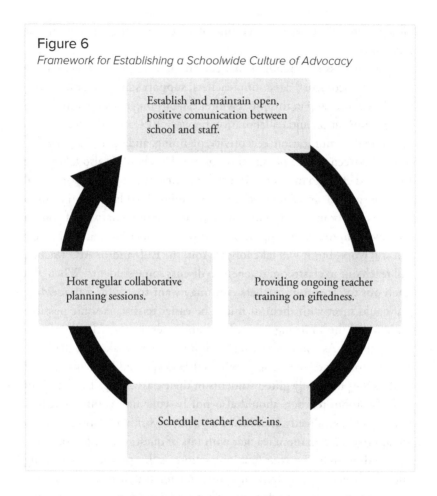

Figure 6
Framework for Establishing a Schoolwide Culture of Advocacy

Establish and maintain open, positive comunication between school and staff.

Providing ongoing teacher training on giftedness.

Schedule teacher check-ins.

Host regular collaborative planning sessions.

Building Relationships With Families of Gifted ELLs

Establishing relationships with families and parents is the next foundational step in extending a culture of advocacy. This step entails building connections and filling any gaps in parents' understandings of giftedness for a child. It also depends on the extent of a teacher's knowledge of the students. For example, some students may only have one parent or may live with their grandparents. Other students may live in a multifamily household with limited access to Internet or a phone.

Table 2
Extending the Culture of Advocacy Schoolwide Step by Step

Step	Definition	What This Looks Like	Nonexamples
Establish and maintain open, positive communication between school staff.	When two or more teachers come together to discuss the needs and strengths of students to create a learning plan for students.	Sharing and/or listening to observations about students' work within a lesson/activity for potential giftedness. It may also include asking for ideas or feedback for future lessons.	Sending an email every couple of months about your lesson plans and/or units.
Provide ongoing teacher training on giftedness.	Interactive presentations that include (a) background on giftedness, (b) best teaching practices for igniting gifts and talents in students, (c) identifying gifted characteristics in students, and (d) best teaching practices for identified gifted learners.	A well-developed staff training or yearlong book study for educators that explores giftedness, best teaching practices, and includes grapple time for teachers to implement their learning in the classroom.	Putting informational flyers in teacher boxes, leading a 30-minute presentation for the whole staff once a year, or creating a website with information for educators.

Table 2, *continued*

Step	Definition	What This Looks Like	Nonexamples
Schedule teacher check-ins.	Create a schedule that works for all parties to meet regularly (such as meeting the first Tuesday of every month or using FaceTime the last Sunday of every month) to discuss potentially gifted ELLs as well as currently identified gifted ELLs. A formal or informal meeting should take place at least once a quarter, preferably once or twice a month, to discuss teacher observations of potentially gifted ELLs based on student work samples of in-class activities.	Possible comments during check-ins: ▲ "Hey! I wanted to share about some cool things that happened with your students during one of my lessons. While we were discussing the fable 'The Tortoise and the Hare,' your student Jose made some great connections and inferences about the Hare. He also did a great job explaining his thoughts about the Hare's character traits in his written response. Are you noticing some of these similar behaviors in your classroom?" ▲ "Twong has been doing an excellent job in our recent math unit. In our math problems about number combinations, he has been able to regroup and solve using multiple methods. He can even explain his process of thinking using much larger numbers by taking the number apart and using a number line. We haven't even introduced the number line or how to break a number apart to regroup. Do you have any ideas of extension activities for number combinations for kindergartners?"	▲ Discussing centers or small-group plans. ▲ Exchanging greetings and then mostly talking about upcoming lessons or standards. ▲ Sharing lesson plans electronically.

Table 2, *continued*

Step	Definition	What This Looks Like	Nonexamples
Host regular collaborative planning sessions.	▲ A more formal exchange of ideas between educators to create learning plans using best teaching practices to nurture gifts and talents through meaningful classroom activities, such as project-based learning or student-driven activities. ▲ Meeting regularly, such as every other Tuesday morning or after school every other Thursday, as a team to discuss and plan meaningful lessons to spark gifts and talents and include time for teacher observation, data collection, and teacher reflection on students' work. ▲ Planning meetings should happen more regularly than pulse check-ins to make the best usage of teacher's time.	A possible conversation during planning might look like this: **Classroom teacher:** We are planning on covering poetry in our upcoming unit. **AIG teacher:** I have a good resource for creative thinking in poetry: *Jacob's Ladder Reading Comprehension Program.* It would challenge students to think critically about word choice, text organization, and vocabulary. **ELL teacher:** The *Jacob's Ladder* resource would be great for ELLs, too, but you may need to scaffold the activities to ensure that students understand the expectations but can also access the text. Maybe you could start with an easier poem but include the higher level thinking question stems similar to the ones in *Jacob's Ladder?*	▲ Sharing unit planners electronically. ▲ Meeting once a year to share unit planners.

Others may have parents who work multiple jobs with limited availability after school. This knowledge of each student, collected by the teacher, can help when trying to build and foster these relationships. It can determine how you will best communicate with parents, as well as what considerations to take into account, such as scheduling parent events before or after school. For example, you may have to send home a letter invitation to an event that includes pictures and simple vocabulary for families with limited Internet or educational background. Or you may ask to have a phone conference for families with multiple jobs or limited means of transportation. Additionally, you may or may not want to request an interpreter for families with limited English language proficiency. Be sure to ask families in advance if they would prefer an interpreter, because you would not want to assume someone needs an interpreter when they do not. This would send the message that you have already made possibly negative assumptions about their background and/or culture.

Once you have established a strong foundation of communication with the families of gifted or potentially gifted ELLs, extend the culture of advocacy to them. The following is a list of key considerations when establishing this relationship:

- ▶ Don't assume parents or ELLs know the purpose and importance of parent/teacher conferences. Make sure to send home an explanation of the conference, specifically what will be discussed and why it is important to attend, beforehand or with a personal invitation.
- ▶ Have interpreters available during parent/teacher conferences.
- ▶ Provide school social activities that have diverse cultural themes.
- ▶ Offer ways for parents to volunteer in the classroom.
- ▶ Provide opportunities for parents to attend workshops about gifted/talented characteristics they can look for with their child.
- ▶ Help parents to develop enriching learning experiences for their children at home or in the community.
- ▶ Introduce parents to community services that can assist them and their families.

The next chapters will explore how to build upon this culture of advocacy by planning meaningful parent outreach events and information to provide for families of identified or potentially gifted ELLs.

Chapter Summary

This chapter detailed where and how to start the system of support for gifted ELLs. It explored how to start the collaboration process between ELL and AIG teachers, along with the corresponding signs of successful collaboration. Next, it examined teachers' knowledge of students and how to nurture a culture of advocacy within the classroom. Then, it introduced how ELL and AIG teachers can begin extending the culture of advocacy for students within classrooms to the entire school, so that every school member becomes accountable and invested in supporting identified or potentially gifted ELLs. Lastly, it explained how classroom teachers and schools can begin fostering positive parent and family relationships. The next chapter will further build upon this foundation to explore planning meaningful parent outreach events and coplanning effective lessons for potentially gifted ELLs.

Discussion Questions

1. Who are the first two key players in starting the collaboration process for supporting gifted ELLs, and what is their role?
2. What does KOS stand for, and what does it entail?
3. How can you develop and continuously build upon your knowledge of students?
4. How do you create a culture of advocacy in your classroom or school?
5. What are some possible barriers for establishing positive parent or family relationships?

CHAPTER 2

Plan

Creating a Plan for Teaching Gifted ELLs

> "A goal without a plan is just a wish."
>
> —Antoine de Saint-Exupéry

The system of support for identifying gifted ELLs discussed in Chapter 1 is the essential prerequisite to the planning phase for gifted ELLs. This chapter builds upon the skills covered in the previous chapter to plan meaningful parent outreach events, coplan lessons and activities between ELL and AIG teachers, and collaboratively plan with support staff and classroom teachers. Before teachers can plan successful parent outreach events, they should have knowledge of their students and an introductory relationship with parents, including learning how parents prefer to communicate, parents' contact information, and if families will need an interpreter. The collaboration between the ELL and AIG teachers established in Chapter 1 will also be further explored in this chapter. Additionally, the schoolwide culture of advocacy promoted by support teachers and classroom teachers to spark potentially gifted students' talents will be discussed. This chapter's ultimate goal is to educate key players, such as parents, ELL and AIG teachers, and classroom teachers, on how to effectively nurture possible gifts and talents in ELLs in preparation of the identification process.

Planning Parent Outreach Events to Educate ELL Families

"At the end of the day, the most overwhelming key to a child's success is the positive involvement of parents."

—Jane D. Hull

Planning parent outreach events is one of my favorite aspects of teaching. When I began teaching, I was hired as an end-of-year ESL teacher right after spring break. I had just finished my student teaching a few months earlier, and I was determined to make a difference. I spent all of the spring break week setting up my classroom, putting together my own bulletin boards, and making lesson plans. Immediately after that, I planned ways to interact with the families of my new students. I wanted to know more about the students and families that I would be teaching, so I hosted an ice cream social. I sent home invitations with the students a week beforehand and then sent home sticker reminders the day of the event. I was pleasantly surprised when almost half of my parents came out. At the event, I shared a slideshow to introduce myself as well as my plan for the next few weeks. Afterward, I got to meet the parents and the students' other siblings. It was an eye-opening experience to see my students behaving so differently with their families, and it helped me to learn more about them. The event had such a great turnout that it made me want to host another, so 2 weeks later, I did.

Another event, a Mother's Day Banquet, became a staple in my teaching repertoire, and I hosted it for the rest of my teaching years. I asked my ELLs to name a meal that they had seen their mothers cook for them, and then I helped them to write a recipe for that dish. The recipes didn't have to be perfect or exact; the point was for each student to write how they thought their mom made this dish. I then compiled all of my students' recipes to create a cookbook. I ran 50-something copies so that every student would have a recipe cookbook to give to their mom that included their special recipe. I also printed the cover with a blank page in between for the students to write a special note inside for their moms. I rushed to get the cookbooks put together for this event, as I only had about 2 weeks to prepare. I remember running around frantically on the day of the event to make sure all of the books had been completed, copied, assembled, and bound.

The moms showed up for their special Mother's Day surprise the Thursday afternoon before Mother's Day weekend, and they were so excited. My students' faces beamed with pride as their moms read their writing and saw all of their hard work, as well as giggled a bit over how their children explained how they thought some dishes were made. I felt proud and happy that I had made a difference. Years later, I still have students who remember working on their cookbook. Because I always had some students who stayed with me for more than one year, I started a rotation of writing projects that would become gifts for moms for our Mother's Day Banquet. Some years I assigned the cookbook, other years a book of poems, and one year an argumentative essay in which students had to explain why their mom was the best mom in the world. Every year, the moms would arrive, and their children would find their specific literary gift and grin as they handed it to their own moms. Then the kids would get a plate of treats, usually muffins or pastries, and some juice to give to their mom. I still have my copy of the student cookbook from my first year of teaching, and I know some of my students still have theirs, too.

At these events, I would circulate to meet with the parents to discuss their children's academic progress and thank them for all of their hard work. The moms would get to meet with each other, and larger families would gather together to talk with their cousins or aunts and grandmothers. I always made an announcement to thank them for coming and to share any important upcoming information. In later years, I handed out pamphlets on how to support their children at home over the summer and when getting ready for end-of-grade testing. Many parents stayed behind to discuss in greater detail how their children were doing, but I made it a point to speak to every family that attended these events to build that connection. Over the years, that connection grew, and so did families' support for their children's learning.

The following are some additional parent outreach events that I have successfully planned and hosted over the years:

- ELL parent open house,
- literacy games and lunch with dads,
- spooky writer's contest night,
- cultural gallery walk and breakfast,
- reader's theater presentations, and
- school's-out-for-summer readathon.

When ELL families attend these events, make sure to explain and introduce them to ways to be more involved in their children's learning or gifted learning identification. The following are ways to get parents involved in their children's gifted learning pathway, according to the Iowa Department of Education (2008):

- Inform parents of your school/district/state's identification process.
- Host parent workshops.
- Help parents become knowledgeable about the significance of their child being identified as gifted/talented.
- Discuss ways they can support and nurture their child's gifts or talents.
- Teach them how to advocate for their child's right to an equitable and appropriate education.
- When possible, communicate in the home language by requesting interpreters for school events.

How to Plan Meaningful Parent Outreach Events

It's easy to talk about great parent outreach events, but how do you get parents to show up? Many times, the parents who need to attend school events the most are the same ones who never attend. They are the parents of struggling readers, students with behavioral concerns, or students needing extra attention. However, it is possible to have success in building parent relationships, regardless of school setting, whether it

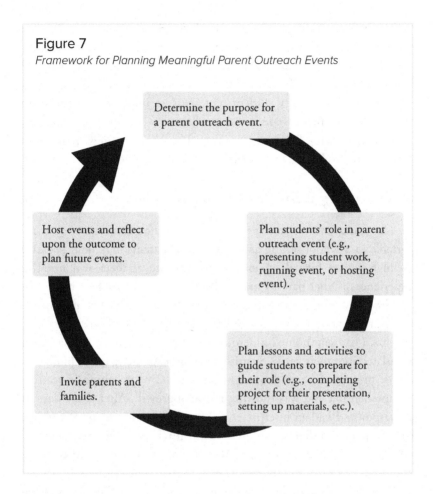

Figure 7
Framework for Planning Meaningful Parent Outreach Events

is a Title I, middle-of-the-road, or high-performing school. The key to high attendance is planning events that are actually meaningful to the parents. It is also important to plan events that are rich in academic content for teachers to share essential insight in their child's learning. Figure 7 is a framework for planning meaningful parent outreach events for all invested key players, including families, teachers, and students.

Another way to get parents to attend an event is to get their children excited or have their children be the stars of the event. For example, teachers can invite parents to the student talent show where their children will be performing and then present an important informational session in the middle of the event, or during intermission, to reach the largest number of families. Other examples would be hosting a reader's theater performance, during which their children will be showing off their reading skills in front of the whole school, or hosting a living wax museum in which every student represents an important person from history. When students are the stars of these events, parents who may otherwise be intimidated or disinterested in school settings are made to feel not only welcome, but also proud of their children.

Empathizing With Parents and Families

As educators, we sometimes forget that not everyone is as comfortable in a school setting as we are. Some parents may hold negative feelings toward formal school settings because of their own negative experiences. Other parents may feel intimidated by teachers if they do not have a strong academic background themselves. I realized this in my fourth year of teaching when I couldn't get a hold of one of my ELL parents. I had sent home numerous invitations and letters that had been translated into their native Spanish language explaining their child's academic progress. The student was more than 2 years behind in reading comprehension and was showing minimal growth. After a few days of no response, I had an interpreter call the family with me on the phone to schedule a conference. At the parent-teacher conference, I learned why the family had not responded to any of our letters: Neither of the parents could read, in any language, and they relied on family friends to help them to complete regular paperwork. I was shocked to learn this, but it greatly impacted my communication with this family. This case highlighted the cultural divide between some families and formal school. For example, the parents had assumed that the letters were just general information, and they trusted the school to do what it thought was best. According to an inquiry of Latino families in California by Musetti (2009), when asked why they didn't complete educational paperwork, the families explained that they trusted teachers to do what is best for their children. From an American educator's perspective, this is shocking because research shows that children learn faster with parent support and reinforcement of literacy skills in the home (Lonigan &

Shanahan, 2009). The example with this family highlighted how both parties—educators and parents—can hold varying and even conflicting views about supporting learners.

Therefore, when planning these parent outreach events, educators should not make assumptions about parents' backgrounds or interests based on myths or misconceptions. Although it may be easy to make assumptions without developing a strong knowledge of students, it is crucial for teachers to recognize their implicit bias. Teachers must always be evolving in their knowledge of students and taking the time to understand where families are coming from as well as their perspectives on education.

In my early years of teaching at a Title I school, I once overheard a group of teachers joking that the students were "too poor to come to school with school supplies but always managed to have the nicest new shoes." At the time, I also recognized this trend, but I did not have the experience or background to understand parents' reasoning behind this choice for their child. As a teacher, I assumed that parents did not care about school and thought that shoes for their children were more important, reaffirming the assumption that the parents thought that school was a waste of their children's time. It was not until later, when speaking with a school social worker, that I came to understand what was happening. The social worker explained that these students lived in areas rampant with crime, including drugs, theft, and violence. Parents in these areas are faced with the difficult challenge of protecting their children, and sometimes it is more important to protect a child's physical safety than offer them educational opportunities. I was confused by this notion until she explained that children who live in these areas often become victims or offenders of these crimes. By having the newest and fanciest shoes, the children are less susceptible to being lured into crime for the visible signs of wealth that drug dealers promise. This realization made me rethink and revisit my original conclusion about the parents of my former students. It's not that they did not care about their children's schooling. They simply had to make the best decision they could for their child. In the case of my students, their parents chose to get the newest shoes to keep them safe.

This example highlights the ways that teachers may not understand some aspects of students' lives and background, and the importance of taking the time to understand families' perspectives about their children's education. Needless to say, in my early years of teaching I held many misconceptions and assumptions that affected my interactions with parents and families. Over the years I learned to reflect upon my implicit bias and to take that bias into account when planning parent outreach events.

Identify the Purpose and Basis for the Parent Outreach Event

In addition to recognizing implicit bias and being cognizant of possible assumptions regarding the families of gifted ELLs, some key considerations that educators must take into account include the following:

▸ What is the purpose of this event, and why do teachers want parents to attend?

▸ What information should teachers provide?

▸ Why will parents want to attend this event? What is the parent buy-in?

▸ What is the best date to hold this event? Are there holidays near this date that may affect the event?

▸ What is the best time for this event? Do most families work later, necessitating a later event? Or are most families available during the school day, possibly in the morning?

▸ What will students' roles be for this event? Will they be presenting or sharing a project, or will they not be expected to attend?

▸ What do teachers need to do to prepare for this event (e.g., send invitations, help students prepare projects, purchase materials such as tablecloths, cups, plates, small snacks, drinks, etc.)?

▸ How many parents or families are expected to attend this event?

▸ How will teachers advertise or encourage families to attend this event (e.g., homework incentive, prizes, free school supplies, or holding this event with a more fun event, like a student talent show)?

This list provides a preliminary framework for designing and planning a meaningful parent outreach event. Once you can effectively answer these questions, it is time to begin planning the details for the event, such as lessons and activities to get students prepared. For example, if students will be performing or presenting information, create a timeline of lessons to ensure that student work is complete before the event. My first year of hosting the Mother's Day Banquet, I was frantically binding the cookbooks only minutes before the event. This is not the ideal situation for a parent outreach event because you want to exude professionalism and knowledge. This is hard to do if it looks like a tornado just hit as you run around preparing for the event right in front of families. The planning stage of the event is crucial.

Creating a Timeline for the Parent Outreach Event

Figure 8 outlines the next few steps of the planning process for a meaningful parent outreach event. Give yourself room in the timetable for students to prepare their project or presentation in case students are absent, as well as to help slower and/or struggling learners. Next, decide how to advertise or invite parents to the event. Some ideas may include a personal letter invitation similar to a party invitation, a parent email blast, phone calls, a parent newsletter, a school/teacher website, or stickers/student wristbands. Of course, the best advertisement comes from students talking to their parents about how excited they are about the event. This is why you will want children to be an integral part of your event. If you send home invitations with an RSVP section, do this 1–2 weeks beforehand, and then send home another reminder the day before the event in case families have forgotten. Lastly, prepare for the event itself. For morning events it may help to set up the night before by putting out vinyl tablecloths, programs, and information packets. Depending on the event, I usually set up some small decorations, such as flowers for Mother's Day, balloons for game night, or a red carpet for the reader's theater. The day of the event, I always include some form of food. For the Mother's Day Banquet, a morning event, I provide muffins and juice. For reader's theater, I prepare small paper bags of popcorn. At open house I provide mints to thank families for their "commit-mint"

Figure 8

Timeline for Planning Meaningful Parent Outreach Events

1–4 MONTHS BEFORE EVENT

Identify the purpose of the parent outreach event. Plan lessons and unit for student activities in preparation of event.

1–2 WEEKS BEFORE EVENT

Start advertising event. Send home parent invitations.

1–2 DAYS BEFORE EVENT

Send home event reminders for parents and families, purchase any food items for event, arrange student work for event, and set up any event decor (e.g., tablecloths, slide shows, programs).

DAY OF EVENT

Set out food items and trash receptacles. Make sure to greet and speak with every family.

AFTER EVENT REFLECTION

Identify what went well and areas for improvement for future parent outreach events.

to their children's learning. Offering free food helps families feel welcome and shows that you appreciate all that they do to help support their children. After the event, reflect on what went well and why, as well as what areas could be improved for the future. For example, did a smaller number of families show up than had responded, or did you run out of food because more families showed up than anticipated? If not as many families showed up as had responded, you may consider how far in advance the RSVP was sent and whether or not students were excited about the event. Also, was the date and time of the event best for families? Could the reminder slips be improved? This knowledge will help you to plan future parent outreach events.

Another key consideration is the frequency of parent outreach events. This should be determined by teachers and administrators who understand families and their ELLs' learning needs. For example, planning an event for every week of the school year would cause teacher burnout and decrease overall attendance. On the other hand, planning only one event a year is not enough to provide parents with information to support their gifted ELLs. Therefore, be sure to consider how often you want to host events. In addition, planning events in conjunction with other large school events, such as talent shows, book fairs, game nights, and musical performances, would be beneficial. I typically host one parent outreach event per quarter. The events are held on various days of the week and at different times, so that if a family cannot make it to one event, then they can probably attend another. I also present the schedule of parent outreach events for the school year in August at open house when most families come to school to meet the new teachers. This lets families plan out whether or not they are able to attend the event with plenty of notice. Parent outreach events are a crucial part of creating a plan to support potentially gifted and identified ELLs. For these events to be particularly meaningful for parents, collaboration between additional support staff and classroom teachers helps. The next section explores how ELL and AIG teachers can collaborate to plan meaningful lessons as well as how ELL and AIG teachers can plan with classroom teachers.

Coplanning Lessons or Units
Between ELL and AIG Teachers

"Without leaps of imagination, or dreaming,
we lose the excitement of possibilities.
Dreaming, after all, is a form of planning."

—Gloria Steinem

The planning process to support potentially gifted ELLs starts with close collaboration between the ELL and AIG teachers before it can extend to classroom teachers. Moreover, before ELL and AIG teachers can begin coplanning lessons, activities, or units, there must a solid foundation for communication and collaboration, as referenced in Chapter 1. If the necessary groundwork has previously been laid, this is the stage when the ELL and AIG teachers start sharing resources and lesson or unit ideas, and possibly coplanning lessons. This stage may look different from school to school, district to district, and state to state, based on each teacher's role within their position. For example, at some schools, ELL teachers are only used for remediation, meaning that they only work with the lowest-performing ELLs, while the higher performing ELLs remain in the classroom. If this how your school, district, or state uses the ELL teacher, this collaboration process can still work. The ELL teacher may not directly teach the lesson with extension activities for the more proficient ELLs, because they are in the classroom, but they can teach those extensions with the remedial students and provide classroom teachers with these same extensions to use inside the classroom. On the other hand, the AIG teacher may be in a similar situation, in which they pull out only identified gifted learners, meaning that they too would need to provide classroom teachers with extension activities for students who do not receive direct support from the ELL or AIG teacher. This means that the ELL and AIG teachers must be in close collaboration and able to plan regularly to develop these extensions. Figure 9 presents a graphic of the interconnection between the ELL and AIG teachers, as well as how it directly correlates to the academic achievement of poten-

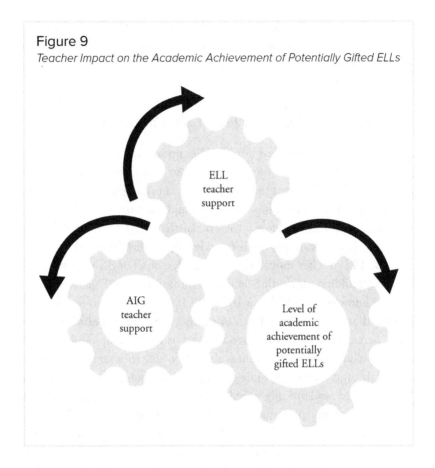

Figure 9
Teacher Impact on the Academic Achievement of Potentially Gifted ELLs

tially gifted ELLs. This section will explore instructional approaches that are beneficial for any learner, not just ELLs or gifted learners.

Coplanning between the ELL and AIG teachers can take the form of informal check-ins or a regular scheduled time once a week or every other week. My AIG teacher and I worked best with informal and impromptu meetings. Due to the close proximity of our classrooms, most of our meetings started by yelling across the hallway to see if the other had a minute for a quick question. We would then walk over to discuss the topic at hand. Meetings do not need to be formal or contrived. If you need to meet, you meet; if you don't, you don't. Our first year working together, we only exchanged a few ideas or proposals. But as the years went by, we got closer and knew each other's resources. We also knew that we could pop over to discuss an upcoming unit or idea to get feedback. Our fluid exchange of ideas and resources took time and nurturing.

The Role of the ELL Teacher in the Planning Stage

This stage of the process heavily relies upon the ELL teacher, particularly to identify potentially gifted ELLs, so that they may get the students identified. Without the support of a knowledgeable ELL teacher, many gifted ELLs are going unnoticed and, in turn, are left without necessary support. Therefore, it is crucial that the ELL teacher knows how and what to look for when considering potentially gifted ELLs.

The ELL teacher should have knowledge of all of the current ELLs in their building, including language proficiency and general background knowledge of ELLs. A strong ELL teacher will have additional insight about each of their ELLs, including academic standing, reading level, parent involvement, classroom teacher relationship, and learning style, to name a few. ELL teachers should be able to interact with ELLs to identify and nurture possible gifts and talents before the student may be considered academically gifted. This makes the ELL teacher the first line in identifying potentially gifted ELLs, along with the classroom teacher. However, most ELL teachers receive little to no training on gifted learning. Research suggests that most teachers have only one course on exceptional children that typically focuses on traits rather than how to support them (Tomlinson, 2014). This highlights a clear need for teachers, particularly ELL teachers, to learn more about gifted learning. Data-driven instruction is crucial in supporting gifted ELLs. Before any teacher can effectively teach a group of students a concept, they should have an understanding of the students' abilities with that topic. The same is true for ELL teachers; they must understand students' potential talents to design effective lessons. But how can an ELL teacher collect and study data to identify possible giftedness if they don't know what to look for? This is where the collaboration with the AIG teacher comes into play.

The Role of the AIG Teacher in the Planning Stage

The AIG teacher's role in this stage is to ensure that the ELL teacher has a clear understanding of what giftedness may look like in classroom settings. This will help the ELL teacher to "catch" possibly gifted learners early on to nurture and develop these talents in preparation for the identification process. Before an ELL can get to the AIG side of their learning journey, the ELL teacher must have seen this potential and helped them to reach and fulfill the necessary criteria for identification. For this reason, when the ELL and AIG teachers meet, the ELL teacher will need to have an excellent understanding of students' abilities. After the ELL teacher explains the students' data, the AIG teacher may offer insight about those observations. For example, if the ELL teacher consistently observes one student who is always asking questions about the text that are more insightful than those of their peers, this would be a key detail to share with the AIG teacher. Other examples may include students with extraordinary leadership skills, deductive reasoning, sense of humor, unique perceptions as seen in their writing or art, or a rapid pace for learning new content. When the ELL teacher shares this information with the AIG teacher, they may ask more questions or offer some additional probes for the ELL teacher to implement with the ELL. Figure 10 shows a visual breakdown of this process.

I typically begin this work in kindergarten, as I am able to quickly identify students with unique talents. With that in mind, it is important to know the difference between students who are gifted and those who are bright in order to ensure that support and resources go to the students that most need them. Janice Szabos (1989) is famously known for creating a table with these distinctions in *Gifted Child Quarterly*. The table presents a list of attributes that can be observed in children, but also makes a distinction between what the characteristics look like for a bright child compared to a gifted child. This table can be used as reference guide for ELL teachers looking to learn more about indicators for bright and gifted learners. However, this list should be used as a reference, not a definitive resource for identifying gifted students. This is particularly true because both bright and gifted students should receive extension activities (Peters, 2016). The AIG teacher is responsible for

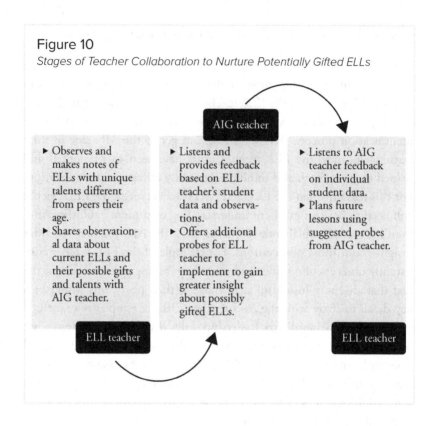

Figure 10

Stages of Teacher Collaboration to Nurture Potentially Gifted ELLs

making sure the ELL teacher is aware of what to look for when working with younger students, as well as how these talents may manifest in the classroom setting. Chapter 3 will explore these characteristics in greater detail.

Coplanning for the ELL and AIG Teachers

Once the ELL and AIG teachers have identified some potential talents in ELLs, or even if they haven't observed any potential talents, the two may begin planning how to nurture current or future talents of students. The purpose of this planning is to build upon students' talents and to foster creative and challenging thinking in students in grades K–2, as well as for older students in grades 3–4. Addressing these potential talents at an early age sets students up for success in later years.

In most cases, the area that potentially gifted ELLs will need the most support in is writing. This is the typical last domain of language proficiency, and it is accordingly the last for ELLs to obtain. Proficiency is reached in the other domains, such as listening, speaking, and reading, before writing.

All of this makes writing the area of greatest impact for nurturing potential talents. Additionally, by adding writing to any content area lesson, rigor is bolstered. For example, if students are learning about different animal features by reading various texts about animals, a great extension activity would be for students to create their own book to compare animal features. This example incorporates the element of creativity by letting students choose their animals for research, as well as which features they would like to compare, such as eyes or habitat. This example also integrates critical thinking into students' learning, as students must synthesize their newly gained information to create a new text of their own. Ideal writing tasks should not be at a lower level of thinking, such as reading a text and answering a text-dependent question; this type of thinking, although important for reading comprehension, does not always integrate critical or creative thinking. Ideal writing opportunities should incorporate creativity, critical thinking, and problem solving. Some examples may include a spooky writing contest, writing a new story using characters from other fiction works, or creating how-to texts. The purpose of these opportunities is to extend students' thinking about topics and let their imagination wander. They are also a great way to identify possible talents in gifted learners, as the writing of gifted learners may be distinctly different from that of their peers (i.e., more detailed storylines, vivid vocabulary, or multiple examples of problem solving).

To support ELLs in this process, I provide time for my students to think, during which no one is allowed to talk, so that they can form their ideas. Figure 11 shows a visual of the process that I use for supporting ELLs in the writing process. After providing think time, I then provide time for my ELLs to share their ideas with a partner and further develop their thoughts. By sharing their ideas aloud, ELLs may organize their thoughts and practice difficult vocabulary before they have to write. I then provide ample work time for students to transition their thoughts

Figure 11
How to Support ELLs in the Writing Process

PREWRITING

▸ **Think time:** Set a timer for students to think about what they want to write without talking or writing (1–5 minutes depending on age).
▸ **Share time:** Provide students with time to share their ideas for their writing with a partner. Make sure partners ask questions and offer meaningful feedback to the author about their ideas.
▸ **Organize time:** Guide students to organize their ideas for their writing using a graphic organizer. Make sure to confer with students during this time.

WRITING

▸ **Work time, conferring, and mini-lessons:** Confer with students one-on-one or in small groups to teach lessons as appropriate to the needs of individual students writing and to offer meaningful feedback.
▸ **Editing, revising, and publishing:** Guide students to partner with at least two peers to read, edit, and offer feedback for revisions. Afterward, students can begin publishing their work.

SHARING

▸ **Sharing completed project and feedback:** Celebrate students' completed written product either through a read aloud to the class or by putting their text on display. Provide opportunities for peer feedback and questions.

and ideas into a graphic organizer as I confer with them one-on-one. After they have completed their graphic organizer, and I have offered feedback, I guide students to begin writing their stories. I always stress the importance of just getting their ideas on the paper. I never worry about spelling, grammar, or syntax at this stage. For my students, the goal is to expand thinking and creativity, so I don't want to do anything that may stifle their ideas.

Additionally, during work time, noticing trends in students' needs can help the teacher plan appropriate lessons. For instance, if multiple students are struggling with run-on sentences, it would be worthwhile to plan a mini-lesson just for those students that explicitly teaches how to split sentences to make their ideas clearer and better understood by the reader. Other topics for mini-lessons may include punctuation, adding adjectives or descriptive details, adding transition words, author's perception, or figurative language. When these skills are explicitly taught, especially in smaller groups, challenging writing concepts are broken down and become meaningful for the individual writer. To teach these mini-lessons, introduce the topic, model how to use the skill in a sample text, and then give students time to practice with the teacher and/or partners. Then, transition to letting them practice with their own text, possibly with you or a peer partner. The grapple time of the mini-lesson is crucial for students to understand and be able to apply the newly gained skill in their own writing.

Next, teach students how to edit and revise their work by having others read it. I usually reference an editing and revising checklist for my students. It always includes checking for punctuation, if the word choice makes sense, and if the reader can understand the story. After students have had their work checked by at least two others, I let them "publish" their writing by rewriting it nicely and neatly on a new paper. If you are fortunate to have one-to-one technology, students can publish their writing on a classroom blog or student website.

Finally, students get the opportunity to share their work by reading it aloud to others or posting it on display. This is a time of celebration for students to see their work and to receive feedback from others, including questions about certain choices or predictions about what the readers think may happen next. This final stage teaches students the cyclical process of reading and writing, specifically how they read to be entertained, informed, or persuaded, and how to use this knowledge to guide future writing activities. Writing also fosters the necessary skills to be a critical and creative thinker. Supporting ELLs in the writing process is especially important because it builds their vocabulary through application and bolsters their self-esteem and self-confidence.

It may be meaningful for the ELL and AIG teachers to coplan a writing or creative thinking unit to see how students interact with higher order thinking concepts. This depends on both teachers' roles and the teaching dynamic of your school, district, or state. Additional ideas of possible lessons or units are explored in Chapter 4.

Planning With Classroom Teachers

"Coming together is a beginning, staying together is a process, and working together is success."

—Henry Ford

The purpose of this section is to prepare the classroom teacher to foster and nurture gifts and talents of ELLs. As important as the ELL teacher is to this role, the classroom teacher is equally important because they spend the most time with these students across multiple subject areas. Therefore, classroom teachers must be equally aware of best teaching practices and methods. This section will explore how classroom teachers can implement the best teaching practices for gifted ELLs, how to meet the needs of gifted ELLs, how to set goals in collaboration with the student, and best teaching strategies for gifted ELLs. It will explain how classroom teachers can plan meaningful lessons to best target gifted ELLs while also providing researched-based practices that are beneficial to all types of learners.

Best Teaching Practices for Gifted ELLs

At this point, as a classroom teacher, you have created a culture of advocacy and developed a broad but deep knowledge of your students. The next step in the process is to develop and plan lessons that may spark or ignite gifts and talents. To help with this process, Figure 12 shows how all three educators can come together to consider the fol-

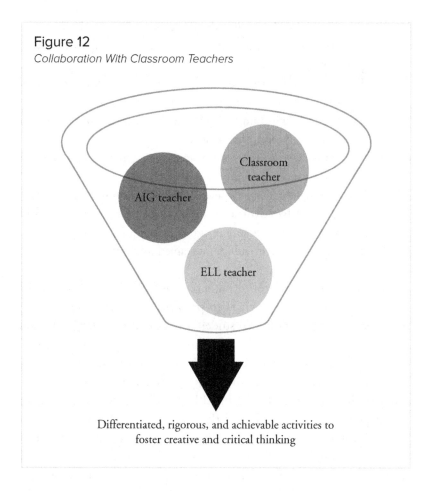

Figure 12
Collaboration With Classroom Teachers

Classroom
teacher

AIG teacher

ELL teacher

Differentiated, rigorous, and achievable activities to
foster creative and critical thinking

lowing best practices for teaching gifted ELLs (Stambaugh & Chandler, 2012):

- ▸ Scaffold instructional content using graphic organizers and tiered levels of questioning.
- ▸ Maintain high levels of expectations in lieu of remedial or deficit lines of thinking. Students must be exposed to higher levels of thinking tasks instead of remedial because they will not reach the higher level if they are not exposed to it. This is otherwise known as the self-fulfilling prophecy, in which teachers assume that students from lower socioeconomic groups cannot per-

form at higher levels and therefore never provide higher level activities; in turn, the students never have the opportunity to perform.

▸ Provide opportunities for students to develop efficient written and oral skills in content areas through teacher modeling.

▸ Provide teaching training on the use/application of accelerated curriculum and modified instructional strategies.

▸ Facilitate opportunities for students to grapple with student choice and real-world problem solving.

▸ Incorporate student goal setting and self-monitoring.

▸ Use content-based preassessments to differentiate or scaffold instructions and measure progress through postassessments.

▸ Provide effective curriculum for trained teachers of gifted learners.

When planning lessons for potentially gifted ELLs, it is beneficial to work with a team of teachers to problem solve, avoid reinventing the wheel, and offer additional student or content knowledge. A good method is to plan as a grade level for content areas. When teams create long-range lesson plans, the ELL and AIG teachers can offer suggestions regarding support and extension thinking. This requires the prerequisite work from Chapter 1. If your ELL or AIG teachers are unable to attend planning, you could send them an email with your unit outline asking for a time to meet to discuss ways to support and extend student thinking within the unit. Based on insight from the ELL and AIG teachers, teams can refer to Figure 13 to ensure that units and lessons meet essential criteria. The outlined criteria require that teachers consider students' individual learning needs and learning styles in the planning process prior to the implementation of the unit. Teacher teams, with the support of the ELL and AIG teachers, can evaluate students' cultural viewpoints by accessing student's prior knowledge and connecting that knowledge with new content and its relevancy to the real world. According to Aguirre (2003), cultural viewpoints play a large role in the underrepresentation of ELLs in gifted programs because of differences in learning styles and different cultural values. By building upon students' schema and differentiating the lessons, key details that

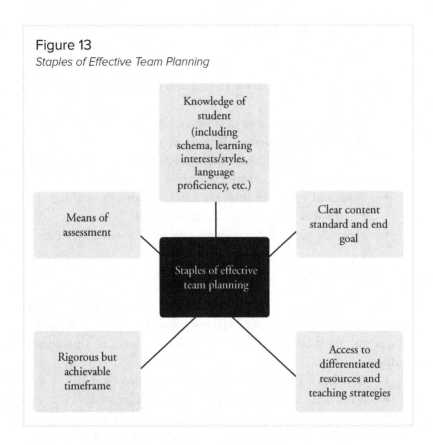

Figure 13
Staples of Effective Team Planning

make learning meaningful and relevant become clear. These key practices serve as the curricular foundation in this planning process.

Additionally, planning meaningful lessons with the collaboration of support staff ensures that the needs of all students have been met. The following is a list of guiding questions for team planning:

- ▸ How are all students' needs being met?
- ▸ Does the pacing of the lesson support all student needs (students performing below grade level, students needing extensions, and students on grade level)?
- ▸ Is the format of the lesson utilizing best teaching skills and strategies for gifted ELLs?
- ▸ Are the activities of the lesson differentiated or scaffolded as needed for students' learning needs?

▸ Is there a clear and realistic mastery goal of the lesson based on students' proficiency levels?

In addition, teachers can use this list of reflective questions to guide future planning:

▸ Were students able to demonstrate mastery with the skills or content from the lesson? Why or why not?
▸ What should be the next steps based on the data of this lesson?
▸ How can this lesson be improved for future groups?
▸ What did you learn from the lesson assessment, and how will you use this information moving forward?
▸ How can you collaborate more effectively moving forward?

Meeting the Needs of Potentially Gifted ELLs

After considering teaching practices, the next step is considering how to meet the needs of gifted learners. The following are needs/conditions that must be met for gifted learners to thrive in an academic setting:

▸ Establish a safe and welcoming learning environment.
▸ Build upon students' background knowledge.
▸ Front-load and explicitly teach content vocabulary.
▸ Utilize high-quality resources, including texts across varied reading levels (Kitano & Pedersen, 2002).
▸ Set high and achievable expectations (Hammond, 2015).

In addition, teachers must foster a supportive "Warm Demander" teacher rapport (Hammond, 2015). Gifted ELLs need to feel that their teacher encourages and supports them because they believe in their ability. This reinforces the work of establishing a culture of advocacy and pioneers the development of cultural competency (Abellán-Pagnani & Hébert, 2012). Research shows that by valuing the cultures and languages of ELLs within an educational context, academic gains will be made (Hammond, 2015; Jiménez, 2017). This occurs because ELLs feel safe, valued, and challenged by a teacher who holds them to a high standard but also provides the necessary supports for success (i.e., "This work will be challenging, but I believe in you, and I am here to support you along the way because you will be successful").

Hammond's (2015) Warm Demander is not developed overnight. It requires the teacher to develop a relationship and continuously build upon it. A Warm Demander consistently establishes the perfect balance between having high expectations and supporting their students. They know when and how to be forceful, as well as how to balance warmth and distance. An authoritarian demands perfection, while the Warm Demander expects greatness. The Warm Demander must not to be too warm or make excuses for students' low performance. Instead, they inspire students to strive for greatness. A Warm Demander never waters down thoughts or ideas for colleagues or students. They always believe that students can do the work. In turn, students always do the work because they trust and know that the teacher will be there to support them along the way.

Establishing and developing all of these teaching strategies takes time and teaching experience. For new teachers, especially first-year teachers, I would only suggest working on 1–3 of these strategies so that you can become an expert at them. In this case, it is better to be really good at a few teaching strategies than just knowledgeable about a lot of strategies. More experienced teachers may already be using quite a few of these strategies but can likely become stronger in one of them. One way to do this would be to choose 2–3 strategies to work on per quarter or even per semester. This breaks the skills into bite-sized, achievable teaching goals.

Setting Goals for Gifted ELLs

Setting goals allows individuals to determine where they want to go and how they want to get there. Goals can be big or small, as determined by the individual. However, the best goals for students are ones that are SMART, or specific, measurable, achievable, relevant, and timely. This means that a good goal for students should be something that is important to them, that allows them to see their progress, and that they can reach within an outlined timeframe. Student goals should be designed in collaboration with students so that they have choice over what they want to work on, how they want to improve in that area, and when they want to have reached this goal. My favorite way to do this is by conferring one-on-one with my students and presenting them with data that include some areas of strength and areas for improvement. Based on that feedback, my students choose one of the areas for improvement and then think about how they want to improve upon that skill. A conversation may look like this:

Teacher: Wow! You did a great job word solving so many words in today's text. You were able to clearly read tough words like *stumbling* and *irreplaceable*. That is a very impressive skill—to be able to solve big words like that while you are reading. I also noticed that you missed or misread a few words that you typically know how to read, such as *happy* and *whenever*. This could be because you are working so hard to read and decode harder words that when you get to easier words, you just guess based on the first letter or other clues. This tells me that you are working to read a higher level text, but it is causing you to struggle with words that you otherwise would know. I have some ideas for a good goal for you, but what do you think would be a good reading goal?

Student: I think that I did a good job on those harder words but that I missed those easier words. I think a good goal could be practicing more sight words or maybe trying books that are a little easier?

Teacher: I think that would be a great goal! Maybe we could put those two ideas together so that you could rotate between reading a harder book and an easier book. For easier books, you could work on your fluency, while on the harder books, you can work on slowing down to self-correct, meaning that as you read, you think. Does that make sense? If something doesn't make sense, then you should go back to reread it. By rotating between higher level and comfortable-level books, you will be able to decode harder words while also making sure you correctly read words you know. What do you think would be a good timeline for this goal?

Student: I think maybe you could listen to me read again by the end of the week or next week to see if I am doing better?

Teacher: That sounds like a great idea! Can you tell me what your goal is for next time?

Student: I am working on rotating between easy books and harder books to become better at self-correcting while reading so that I can catch myself if I read a word incorrectly. We will check my progress either later this week or next week.

Teacher: That is correct and excellent! Can you please write down your goal on your sticky note bookmark so that we both come back prepared? Great job!

This example shows how students can make inferences about their own learning needs based on teacher feedback, as well as how students can problem solve to identify their next learning steps. It also highlights how students can take ownership of that goal by choosing a follow-up timeframe for the goal, repeating it to the teacher, and recording their goal for easy reference. Having students choose their area of need, based on teacher feedback, gives them choice and ownership over their own learning. This shows students that you care but that they are responsible for their own growth toward this goal.

The following is a list of research-based goals for gifted ELLs to maximize their learning potential, based upon a literature review by Kitano and Pedersen (2002). These are examples of areas of feedback that teachers can provide for students to help them choose and set their own learning goals:

- ► **Language proficiency:** Gifted ELLs should demonstrate higher growth gains than other peers with similar language backgrounds. For example, a gifted learner with a year of learning English should show higher growth gains compared to a typical peer who has also been learning English for a year.

- ► **Level of thinking or Depth of Knowledge:** Gifted ELLs should be able to demonstrate a higher level of thinking compared to their peers (Kitano & Pedersen, 2002). A goal for a gifted ELL may include demonstrating a higher level of understanding and application of the scientific method, if they are studying science, by proposing a question for research and designing a scientific experiment that they implement. A literacy goal to show depth of knowledge may include charging first-grade students to use their knowledge of fairy tales to create an original play with characters from at least two fairy tale stories. This task requires the students to understand those characters and how they would interact around other characters.

- ► **Quantity or quality of details:** Gifted ELLs should be able to demonstrate a higher attention to detail in content areas of interest. This may include an ability to organize, graph, or draw specific renderings of key details. A good goal for a gifted ELL, within a unit, may be to demonstrate their level of understanding of a concept by creating or evaluating a visual product pertaining to the content. An example may include creating an anchor chart on the scientific method or on how to use character traits to draw conclusions about a character using key details from the text.

- ► **Content-specific goals:** Research indicates that ELLs may more easily reach higher goals in mathematics, science, and research skills than in literacy. For example, they may not be writing at grade level in third grade but should be on grade level in reading and writing by fifth grade. This could make setting a math, science, or literacy goal appropriate for a gifted ELL. The math or science goal would include above-grade-level extensions, whereas the literacy goal would include higher order thinking using appropriate texts for current reading level.

After students and teachers collaboratively choose a learning goal with a follow-up date, teachers should check back in with students to discuss progress. At the follow-up meeting, it may be determined that a student needs more time to practice because they have not reached their goal, or the student may demonstrate mastery of their goal and therefore need guidance in choosing a new goal. The follow-up meetings are crucial in the goal-setting process because they hold students accountable. Also, if students think that their teacher doesn't care about their goals, then students will learn to stop caring about their learning goals, too.

Teaching Strategies for Gifted ELLs

In addition to best teaching practices, there are a number of teaching strategies that can support teachers to plan and implement meaningful lessons. Similar to the teaching practices listed previously, it is better to be strong in a select few strategies than knowledgeable about all of them but unable implement them into lessons. The following are comprehensive and research-based best teaching strategies for reaching gifted ELLs:

- ▸ **Access and build upon student background knowledge:** Assess children's interests and background knowledge (e.g., favorite books, hobbies, etc.). Build upon background knowledge or front-load units using visuals, mixed media, and realia (e.g., suspenseful pictures prior to reading a mystery). Explicitly teach how to make connections with a text using prior knowledge.
- ▸ **Show rather than tell:** Show visuals, maps, photos, pictures, videos, and graphic organizers to further student understanding. Gersten and Baker (2000) noted that visuals, such as concept

and story maps, compare/contrast thinking sheets, and graphic organizers, reinforce concepts and vocabulary acquisition.

▸ **Confer with gifted ELLs:** Schedule times to individually confer with gifted ELLs on specific strategies that they can use to support their learning. This allows the students to receive the necessary feedback in a format that may otherwise be embarrassing if addressed in a whole-class situation. Kitano and Pedersen (2002) shared an example of a child who may struggle to comprehend or to read with expression, but who can decode. The teacher may choose to meet with that student one-on-one. During that conferring time, the teacher may model read a text with notable punctuation to show how to read with expression for the first sentence before allowing the student to practice with the next sentence as the teacher listens. Fluent readers might be offended by this approach, but when used one-on-one with the gifted ELL, the social and peer anxiety is removed.

▸ **Facilitate student learning teams:** Allow opportunities for students to ask and answer peer questions related to literacy skills. These learning teams may be teacher-selected or student-selected depending on the desired outcome. For example, allowing students to choose their own team creates a level of comfort for gifted ELLs, as they may choose peers they feel more comfortable sharing with—a good choice if the topic is already challenging and you want to target verbal expression skills. If the topic is less challenging and you want to incorporate more higher order thinking, choose the learning teams for students to ensure a higher level of academic questioning among peers.

▸ **Read aloud, think aloud:** Teach using the read aloud, think aloud strategy to model how good readers think while reading. In this strategy, the teacher says what they are thinking while they read. For example, when reading the fable of the tortoise and the hare, you might pause to say "Hmm . . . that hare sure does act and sound like a bully, but I wonder why it doesn't seem to bother the tortoise?" This example helps students to start making connections about those characters, consider the characters' traits, make predictions and inferences, and draw conclusions. To take it further, you might add, "I wonder how I would describe the tortoise," or "This reminds me of . . ." or "I think the hare is a bully because he makes fun of others while he chants that he is the fastest animal." These statements, modeled while reading, show students what and how they could be thinking as they are reading on their own (Jiménez, 2017). For example, you might model struggling to decode a word by substituting different sounds within that word until you find the correct word through trial and error. The correct sentence may be: *The tortoise meandered along the path, while the hare easily sped far ahead out of sight.* While reading, you might mispronounce *meandered* to model how to decode, or stop to think aloud, "I wonder what *meander* means? Maybe it means to walk slow, or it could mean to walk around, because the tortoise is walking slowly around on the path. I can see the path is long and winding, but the hare is way ahead." This teaches students how to solve for unknown words by using context clues, such as pictures, to help their understanding of the text.

- ▶ **Use multiple critical thinking and higher order thinking strategies:** Some suggested strategies include:
  - ▷ Socratic seminar (Ball & Brewer, 2000),
  - ▷ problem-based learning (Stepien & Pyke, 1997),
  - ▷ tiered instruction (Tomlinson, 2014),
  - ▷ multiple intelligences (Gardner, 1983/2011), and
  - ▷ simulations and/or role-playing (e.g., mock trials, reenactments, wax museums).

- ▶ **Scaffold and differentiate:** Do so as needed, and as appropriate, for each student or student group. For example, you might distribute various-sized sticky notes for children to take notes based on each child's writing proficiency. A more advanced writer may receive a larger note than a newcomer, thus limiting the newcomer's language demands while still requiring the same demonstration of content understanding. In a scenario documented by Kitano and Pedersen (2002), a teacher chose to not differentiate a task but, instead, to differentiate the scaffolding needed for students to complete the task. The task required students to create their own tale by referencing their completed matrix or graphic organizer of the elements of fairy tales. The teacher realized that all of his students were capable of completing this task, although some would need significant guidance or assistance, while others might need little to none, leaving him to work with those with higher needs.

These strategies are beneficial to all types of learners, not only gifted ELLs. Using various teaching strategies helps to support various learning styles and needs.

Chapter Summary

Planning to support gifted ELLs requires that key players have laid the foundation to plan meaningful activities to engage gifted ELLs. The planning process builds upon the relationships established in Chapter 1 to plan meaningful parent outreach events for parents to gain knowledge about how to support their gifted ELL at home. Parent outreach events require detailed planning on the teacher's and school's part to have a high turnout, as well as for parents to gain the information that teachers wish to share. Some of those key considerations include the students' roles at the event, cultural considerations, and having a clear timeline for preparing for the event.

Coplanning between the ELL and AIG teachers builds upon communication and collaboration to share resources and information about students' talents. Collaborating about the needs of individual students creates a system of support for those students to be academically engaged and challenged. It also helps the ELL teacher to begin the necessary nurturing of potentially gifted ELLs' talents, an essential step to casting a wider net for identifying gifted ELLs.

Additionally this chapter explored the role of the classroom teacher to incorporate best teaching practices for gifted ELLs—meeting their needs, setting goals, and planning lessons that integrate various teaching strategies. Presenting classroom teachers with a toolkit of resources allows them to better support gifted ELLs and nurture those potential talents.

Discussion Questions

1. What are some key considerations for planning future parent outreach events?
2. What are some challenges that your school, district, or state faces in planning parent outreach events?
3. Who will be involved in the planning of the process to support gifted ELLs, and what will be their roles?
4. How will potentially gifted ELLs be nurtured in various learning settings (e.g., in the regular classroom, with the ELL teacher, with the AIG teacher, in special areas, at home, etc.)?

CHAPTER 3

Listen

How to Listen and Observe for Potentially Gifted ELLs

> "My fascination with letting images repeat and repeat—or in film's case 'run on'—manifests my belief that we spend much of our lives seeing without observing."
>
> —Andy Warhol

We have all heard the saying that most communication is non-verbal, referring to the importance of body language and vocal tone. Listening to students is not a singular form of data collection completed by just noting students' in-class responses; rather it is a compilation of formative data that a teacher compiles based on their overall knowledge of students. It requires not only listening to students, but also observing their ideas, thought and work processes, motivation, leadership, collaboration, and end products to consider if they are potentially gifted learners. According to Castellano (2003), "many minority students possess special talents that are valued within their own culture; however these special talents are not recognized by the dominant culture as signs of giftedness" (p. 19). Parents and families are the first in line in this listening process because they are the first to recognize that their child is unique or talented in ways different than their peers. The next in line is the classroom teacher, followed by support staff. This chapter will explore how key players, such as parents, classroom teachers, support staff, and administrators, can collaborate to listen and observe for potentially gifted ELLs.

Listen Using Research-Based Characteristics of Gifted Learners

Humans have developed an innate ability to listen to our surroundings for survival purposes. These natural instincts have helped us to survive and avoid potentially dangerous situations. Over time, we have developed these listening skills to interpret, process, and navigate situations using communication. These same skills are the key to observing potential talents, but this requires more than just listening. The most beneficial way to observe and gain insight about a child is to sit beside them. As you sit beside them, you can listen to their thoughts and see their abilities, motivation, interactions, and perception. You can also confer with them to ask questions about their thinking while working on a task or activity or even just playing. Listening and observing a child's potential talents seems easy, in and of itself, but the key is to know what to look for as you are gaining this insight. This section explores the indicators of gifts and talents, as applicable for each key player.

For Parents of Potentially Gifted Learners

> "It is time for parents to teach young people early on that in diversity there is beauty and there is strength."
>
> —Maya Angelou

As a parent, you always want the affirmation that you are doing the right thing and making the right choices for your child, but that can be easier said than done. Every child and every parent is different, and every situation is different for those individuals. This is particularly challenging for parents of gifted children because, unlike with students with learning needs, pediatricians do not offer insight to guide parents in the identification of these talents. Moreover, for parents to recognize their child's potential gifts and talents, they have to seek out the information themselves. For immigrant families arriving in a new country, there are many more immediate concerns, such as financial security, housing, and safety. So how can parents become educated and informed about potential gifts and talents in their children? This section outlines gifted attributes that are considered absolute values or traits of giftedness and gifted behaviors in children. Typical characteristics of giftedness in children, identified by Webb et al. (2007), include:

- ▶ **Strong verbal abilities:** Children are able to communicate effectively, are concerned with word precision, and may have higher comprehension skills in text; this leads to early reading and questioning about texts due to self-motivation.
- ▶ **Unusually good memory:** They enjoy absorbing as much information as possible and are able to quickly retain information with less exposure and repetition than their peers. This may include a photographic memory of a page or visual display.
- ▶ **Intense curiosity:** They are highly inquisitive and want to learn more about the "why" behind most concepts. They may seem impolite to adults or others, but they may not be aware that their line of questioning may be rude.
- ▶ **Wide range of interests:** They are interested in a variety of activities or hobbies, which may be frustrating for teachers or adults who observe numerous partially complete projects, assignments, or activities (e.g., starting a puzzle and walking away to learn the piano, but then joining a chess club). Others may have tunnel vision for a specific interest, such as a coin collection, that includes organizing, counting, and storing items.
- ▶ **Interest in experimenting:** Gifted learners want to know and understand how things go together to create something. This can entail disassembling and reassembling a computer, toaster, or toy. It can also be seen in the mixing of ingredients in a recipe to see how those changes affect the end product.
- ▶ **Passionate imagination and creativity:** This can include imaginary friends, pets, and places that, although imaginary, are very

real for gifted children. Parents and other adults may worry that this imagination is a sign of emotional trauma; however, many adults commonly and widely accept fantasy in worlds of science fiction or mysteries.

▸ **Remarkable sense of humor:** Five- and 6-year-olds may possess an active imagination and a knack for creativity. By 8 or 10, gifted children may develop an unusual sense of humor that may include riddles, wordplay, or puns.

▸ **Desire for reasons and understanding:** They have an innate desire for understanding the purpose behind most customs, traditions, and thinking. They may not realize that their inquisitive view of the world is unique to them (e.g., a child may be surprised that not all kindergartners are able to read a clock to tell time).

▸ **Impatience with others or with themselves:** Gifted children may possess a genuine enthusiasm for learning that can transform into impatience with others who may not grasp solutions to problems as quickly. Additionally, gifted learners may have feelings of frustration with themselves if they clearly visualize something but are unable to produce their idea, possibly due to delayed fine motor skills to build, draw, or write.

▸ **Longer attention span:** Gifted children show signs of longer attention spans compared to their peers. This can be seen in extended reading, building of models, or practicing a hobby such as a piano. Gifted children may hold concentration in these activities for hours by tuning out the outside world.

▸ **Complex thinking:** Gifted children possess a unique ability to organize and develop complex systems or structures. For example, they may be able to reimagine animals by combining them with other animals' features to come up with new animal kingdoms (e.g., the "Mammatilian" Kingdom, a product of large lizards and bears). This search for complexity results in boredom with routine tasks.

▸ **Concern with social or political problems or injustices:** Gifted children actively seek to correct or rectify injustice. This is rooted in their desire to make society "fair" or "just" and can manifest in various ways (e.g., standing up for others being bullied or for the rights of unprotected individuals, such as the homeless, immigrants, or women).

▶ **Sensitivity:** Gifted children have a keen ability to recognize more in their environment than peers. They observe and intellectually understand situations but may not understand their emotional reactions. For example, a gifted child may become upset when they see a homeless family begging or start crying if they hear their parents arguing. This can lead them to be hurt easily by peers as well as to physical sensitivities to touch or smells.

▶ **Intensity:** Gifted children have a strong desire and will to wholeheartedly commit to a task, hobby, or belief. They adamantly express opinions, beliefs, or interests. One mother of a gifted child shared her child's motto: "Anything worth doing is worth doing to excess." If a gifted child loves building, they may only care about their LEGO. This intensity can be seen in tantrums, peer competition, power struggles, sibling rivalry, and even sleep.

▶ **Daydreaming:** Gifted children's intense imaginations can lead to excessive daydreaming, or being lost in their own world of imagination. This can be concerning for adults and teachers, but it can also lead to successful careers in problem solving (pp. 12–18).

These common attributes and characteristics listed of giftedness are well researched. However, what may be considered gifted in one culture may not be in other cultures.

Iowa Department of Education (2008) found these attributes of gifted ELLs:

▶ motivation to learn,
▶ effective communication skills,
▶ effective problem-solving strategies,
▶ high level of insight, and
▶ logical approach to reasoning.

In addition, Castellano (2002) offered the following attributes. Gifted ELLs may:

- eagerly share their culture;
- seek to teach others about their native language and eagerly translate for others;
- have a strong sense of pride in their cultural heritage and ethnic background;
- balance accepted norms between native culture and new culture;
- easily understand jokes and puns;
- read in their native language two grades above their level;
- maintain a linguistic proficiency level above nongifted peers;
- be able to code switch;
- understand the greater global community and have awareness of other cultures and languages;
- learns a second or third language at an accelerated pace;
- excel in math achievement tests;
- demonstrate strengths in the creative areas of fluency, elaboration, originality, and flexibility; and
- demonstrate leadership abilities in nontraditional settings, such as the playground, home, church, clubs, etc.

Finally, Kitano and Pedersen (2002) found that gifted ELLs:

- have excitement for learning;
- show high-level thinking skills, independence in working, eagerness, and enthusiasm;
- enjoy exploring new content but struggle with reading comprehension, idioms, and content-specific vocabulary; and
- show critical thinking and higher ranges of creativity when sharing verbally/orally, but those ideas and/or thoughts may not transfer into their writing.

This is a comprehensive list of common attributes and characteristics of the gifted, but it does not imply that your child must possess all of these characteristics to be gifted. Nor does this list mean that if your child meets all of these criteria they must be gifted. This list serves as a starting point to help parents listen, observe, and seek to understand their child.

As parents, you will notice these talents long before your child begins schooling. You spend the most time around your child before, and even after, they begin school. You may have noticed some of these traits but didn't quite understand what they meant. Knowing and understanding more traits can help you to nurture these talents early on. Supporting your child early on can guide them to understand more about themselves, especially if they are struggling to make friends or feel overly emotional.

The traits and talents listed in this chapter offer a good starting point for recognizing these unique talents to begin nurturing your child's ability. With that in mind, parents should recognize that gifted learners may have additional needs when it comes to processing and understanding. Some of those areas include socioemotional needs; children may feel isolated or different from their peers, experience strong emotions that they may not understand, or struggle with underachievement and perfectionism. According to research, gifted children often hold high expectations of themselves and those around them (Webb et al., 2007). They often want society to match their idealistic views, and when it does not, they may feel pressure to make a significant difference to make the world better. This results in stress and a burdensome challenge, as others around them also expect great things from them. These feelings can manifest into anger, frustration, impatience, and distrust. Discuss these socioemotional needs with your child to help them process their feelings and guide them to realize that what they are feeling is normal. You can build upon this by exploring the usage of bibliotherapy to support gifted learners' socioemotional needs (see Chapter 5).

For Classroom Teachers

"We cannot create observers by saying 'observe,' but by giving them the power and the means for this observation, and these means are procured through education of the senses."

—Maria Montessori

As teachers, you are constantly collecting data to gain more information about your students to guide instruction. This includes formal and informal assessments, observations, projects, exit tickets, progress monitoring, and many other tools. The purpose of student data collection for classroom teachers is to paint a picture of a child's level of understanding and areas for growth. This student picture guides the instructional decision-making process. Data collection, referred to as "listening" in this chapter, helps the classroom teacher to recognize potential gifts and talents. However, because this form of data collection is informal and subjective to each classroom teacher, it can lend itself to bias when teachers are considering who can and who cannot be potentially gifted. Therefore, teachers must remain aware of their own misconceptions regarding this process. Moreover, this stage requires that teachers not only are aware of their implicit bias, but also seek to make a mind shift to recognize potential talents in gifted ELLs. One way to do this is to evaluate your classroom culture using the scale in Figure 14. The purpose of the scale is to identify where you, your classroom, and your students fall when working with ELLs and other underrepresented groups. The scale may also help you to recognize how students treat each other. In positive classroom cultures, ELLs will feel welcome and encouraged to share their family heritage with their peers, whereas in tolerant classroom cultures, ELLs may feel accepted but embarrassed about their family heritage and background. Similarly, ELLs in tolerant and ignorant classroom cultures may seek to hide their language background to fit in and may shy away from supporting other ELLs, for fears of being likened to newly immigrated students, and therefore outsiders. Compared to their peers, gifted ELLs are more aware of their academic abilities and the mistreatment of others (Mun et al., 2016). For this reason, teachers must develop their knowledge of students, as well as continuously strive to cultivate a strong positive cultural learning environment for all learners.

This section explores how gifted indicators may look different in students with varied cultural backgrounds and forms of intelligence, and how teachers can identify potential gifts and talents based on cultural perspectives. For example, in some cultures, students are expected to consume knowledge more passively because it is unacceptable to ask

Figure 14
Classroom Culture Scale

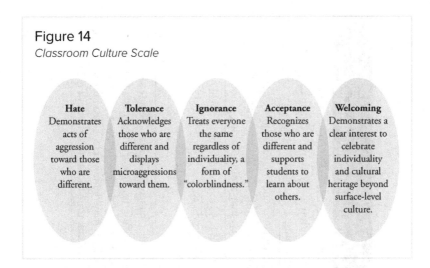

Hate	**Tolerance**	**Ignorance**	**Acceptance**	**Welcoming**
Demonstrates acts of aggression toward those who are different.	Acknowledges those who are different and displays microaggressions toward them.	Treats everyone the same regardless of individuality, a form of "colorblindness."	Recognizes those who are different and supports students to learn about others.	Demonstrates a clear interest to celebrate individuality and cultural heritage beyond surface-level culture.

authority figures questions. This is in contradiction to some of the characteristics of giftedness in American culture, including that gifted learners are very inquisitive. In this example, children from certain cultural backgrounds may be disregarded and not considered as gifted because "inquisitiveness" looks different in their culture. Traditional characteristics of giftedness may manifest in various forms for students who are culturally, linguistically, and ethnically diverse, as traditional forms may not culturally align. For instance, a CLED student may be less inclined to be a risk taker, a common characteristic of giftedness, depending on their cultural background. Furthermore, some teachers may not recognize giftedness across different cultures because of cultural specificity (Stambaugh & Chandler, 2012). Table 3 provides insight into what the characteristics of giftedness may look like through a cultural lens.

Cultural viewpoints and background knowledge can help teachers to recognize the gifts and talents in underrepresented populations, such as Hispanic, Asian, Native American, and African American students. The exploration of cultural values and their impact on giftedness presented within Table 3 serves as a starting point in the consideration and understanding of the role of students' cultural backgrounds within their learning journey toward gifted identification. Teachers may use this table as an introduction to cultural influence on giftedness but are also

Table 3

Characteristics of Giftedness Interpreted Through a Cultural Lens

Gifted Indicators	Applicable Culture	Cultural Values	Cultural Influence on Gifted Characteristics
Strong verbal ability	Hispanic	Traditional language and communication habits formed by family norms and expectations.	Students are able to fluently communicate with peers within the community, including code switching.
	Asian	Tradition of respecting authority figures, including elders.	Students may not make or hold extended eye contact, as this may be viewed as challenging authority; may avoid speaking if not spoken to.
	African	Wide variations in verbal customs across African countries. Male dominance is widely accepted across most African countries.	African boys may speak more openly than African girls. Respect toward elders is very important.
	Native American	Communication customs vary across tribal communities; they have varied value in nonverbal communication and forms of expression.	Possible characteristics may include soft or slow speech patterns, delayed responses, and strong visual-spatial skills within verbal expression; students may demonstrate a need for processing and think time to form methods of expression.

Table 3, *continued*

Gifted Indicators	Applicable Culture	Cultural Values	Cultural Influence on Gifted Characteristics
	Hispanic	Physical and/or spiritual proximity to others is a valued tradition, sometimes known as *abrazo*.	Maintaining emotional and physical support, such as through eye contact and feelings of encouragement, helps students to achieve maximum academic productivity.
	Asian	Limited personal space and physical contact are viewed negatively. Preventing family shame is paramount.	Students may be wary or uncomfortable with physical contact or close proximity to others; may become very emotional regarding criticism, especially if they are publicly admonished in a classroom setting.
Intensity (including emotional and physical)	African	Physical touching/close proximity is a cultural norm that varies across African countries; most cultures dictate a level of distance between different genders (i.e., boys and girls).	Students appreciate feelings of belonging/camaraderie within gender groups (i.e., boys with boys and girls with girls). Eye contact may vary depending on their native region. In some regions, eye contact is welcomed in greetings, whereas in others, eye contact is not permitted by girls/women.
	Native American	Native Americans may place value in active participation after watching and learning. Navajo children learn best using hands-on learning.	Students may accelerate in kinesthetic learning environments. Student self-discipline can lead to perfectionist tendencies.

Table 3, *continued*

Gifted Indicators	Applicable Culture	Cultural Values	Cultural Influence on Gifted Characteristics
	Hispanic	Family structure is very important, including a dynamic male dominance within the family culture.	Hispanic females may be held to a higher standard than male siblings. Hispanic females may have less verbal aggressiveness and personal initiative.
	Asian	Family honor is very important, as well as personal responsibility to positively represent the family.	Asian students may possess a strong sense of self-discipline and self-motivation, including a preference for structure and defined units.
Sensitivity to feelings and expectations of others	African	Family members are judged by each family member's standing, holding true to the belief that a family is as strong as its weakest link.	Students may show positive emotions openly, but negative or aggressive emotions vary across different countries. In some countries it is a form of family embarrassment to show negative emotions, whereas in others, members may express themselves very overtly, to the point that it may look like yelling.
	Native American	Feelings and displays of knowledge are not encouraged in various communities. Tribal communities encourage and embrace personal introspection and reflection.	Students may demonstrate aggressive emotions openly, as well as times of silent reflection to cope with strong emotions. They may emphasize indirect communication (physical stance, facial expressions, eye contact, etc.).

Table 3, *continued*

Gifted Indicators	Applicable Culture	Cultural Values	Cultural Influence on Gifted Characteristics
	Hispanic	The family is a nuclear model that extends to extended family members (e.g., aunts, uncles, cousins, grandparents, etc.).	Hispanic students often assume responsibility for family or younger siblings.
Social justice (*solution-oriented, particularly for social and emotional problems*)	Asian	Various religious influences, such as Confucianism, Buddhism, or Dharma beliefs. Traditional views of social justice may result in the moral exclusion of those who are labeled as deserving of negative consequences.	Asian students may uphold cultural beliefs that social justice is important; however, these beliefs may coincide with beliefs that life is unjust to those who deserve justice.
	African	Varies across countries. Can include tribal traditions of togetherness, importance of family bonds, and the duty to share with each other. Also can include a finite opinion of right and wrong or good and bad.	African students may take on a collective role to work together, share, and offer support to those needing it. They may show a lack of desire to be better or superior to others, and may seek for all students to have opportunities. They may have a strong opinion of what is right or wrong based on cultural norms (e.g., cheating, theft, etc.).
	Native American	Value restorative practices seeking peaceful resolutions and reparative justice practices within tribal communities.	Students may have strong problem-solving skills to restore peaceful balances between students; may also show aggression and impatience toward individuals or groups that demonstrate inconsiderate habits toward others.

Table 3, *continued*

Gifted Indicators	Applicable Culture	Cultural Values	Cultural Influence on Gifted Characteristics
	Hispanic	Uphold traditional family cultural values and norms.	Gifted Hispanics are able to successfully adapt and function in two or more cultures.
	Asian	Selectively strong memory for facts rather than personal events, narrative details, and fictional details.	When compared to other students, Asian students may retain facts as well as other students but tend to retain facts that are more culturally important, such as numerical data or functions.
Good memory	African	Strong memory for personal stories, folktales, religious histories, and customs.	African students may remember explicit details of narratives that tell stories or involve morals or lessons.
	Native American	Cultural emphasis on the value of storytelling and auditory skills to remember and pass down histories and values from generation to generation.	Students may be acculturated to the belief of "watch and learn, then do"; they may learn best through modeling. Student practice time can be viewed as a sign of weakness.

Table 3, *continued*

Gifted Indicators	Applicable Culture	Cultural Values	Cultural Influence on Gifted Characteristics
	Hispanic	Collaborative, rather than competitive. Concerned about the group as a whole rather than beating others, relating to collectivist cultural values.	Students are able to accomplish more and work better when in small-group settings instead of working individually.
Leadership	Asian	May uphold a cultural value known as arugama, or akirame, meaning having a mature sense of self-control or resignation.	Students may regard learning with an air of passivity or lack of assertiveness.
	African	Strong sense of self-confidence and self-esteem as nurtured by family traditions.	Students work well individually or in small-group settings; may exhibit leadership skills in culturally responsive school settings.
	Native American	In various communities, female figures are viewed as dominant within the family structure. Regarded as a collectivist culture.	Students may be humble in their display of knowledge; may prefer to work individually rather than in a group.

Note. Information gathered from Adams & Chandler, 2014; Cline & Schwartz, 1999; Esquierdo, 2006; Ford, 2013; Ford & Grantham, 2003; Gentry et al., 2014; Idang, 2015; Khlystov, n.d.; Melton, 2005; and Wang, 2009.

encouraged to further develop their knowledge of students' cultural traditions and values. Moreover, Table 3 is not intended to be used to represent finite terms of giftedness within these cultures, especially because the table incorporates numerous cultures within varied geographical areas; its conclusions are, therefore, generalizations. Race, although not explicitly covered in the table, also plays a role in how students from various cultures may be perceived. According to Cline and Schwartz (1999), gifted African Americans face many of the same challenges as other gifted peers, including poor peer relations, perfectionism, heightened sensitivity, and high expectations from others. However, these challenges are compounded by societal views, including racism, discrimination, lowered teacher expectation, and high rates of poverty. Moreover, these same negative perceptions result in fewer CLED students being identified for gifted programs. Therefore, it is crucial for teachers to gain insight into their students' cultural backgrounds and histories.

Another key consideration when listening and observing for students' potential gifts and talents is the theory of multiple intelligences (Gardner, 1983/2011). In order for students to show possible signs of multiple intelligences, students need to be exposed to differentiated curriculum content. Because core subjects involve more than one intelligence theory, exposing students to core subjects facilitates opportunities for gifted students to show their abilities.

According to Gardner (1983/2011) there are eight forms of intelligence that can be highly interconnected (see Figure 15). Linguistic intelligence entails special talents in syntax, semantics, and writing or oral abilities. Logical-mathematical intelligence is the ability to maneuver and navigate numbers and reason at a higher degree than peers. The ability to observe, represent, and imagine in various configurations is visual-spatial intelligence. Bodily-kinesthetic intelligence is the ability to move one's body in unique and talented forms, such as gestures, dance, or physical sports. The sensitivity to music, as with composers and/or performers, is musical intelligence. Interpersonal intelligence is the ability to relate to others easily, whereas intrapersonal intelligence is the ability to understand oneself. Naturalistic intelligence is the ability to understand nature and appreciate the environment. When applied to

Figure 15
Theory of Multiple Intelligences (Gardner, 1983/2011)

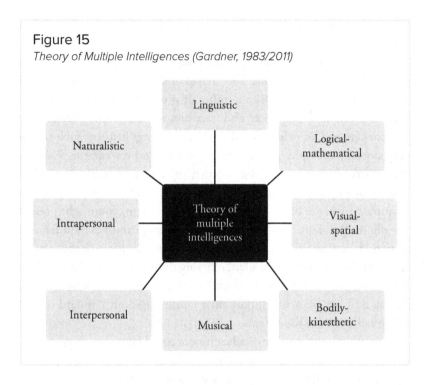

content areas, children have the ability to demonstrate the various forms of intelligence through problem solving and creating to show mastery.

Teachers can incorporate these intelligences into meaningful activities through cross-curricular projects and project-based learning opportunities. Cross-curricular learning opportunities are lessons, projects, or activities that integrate more than one subject area, such as literacy, math, social studies, or science. A cross-curricular project might include a unit using the text *Flat Stanley*, in which students create their own Flat Stanley and send him to visit family members across the world to learn about new areas (Brown & Pamintuan, 2010). Those same families return Flat Stanley with photographs of him visiting new sites, allowing the classroom to interconnect literacy with culture, social studies, geography, and math standards. Students can present about the new sites or cultures that Flat Stanley explored, as well as map the locations of the areas on a world map, along with the sites the other Flat Stanleys visited. To connect math, the teacher can measure the distance to each site and then add up all of the distances to measure the total distance that all Flat Stanleys traveled.

Another cross-curricular project would be for students to create a geometric city using various 3-D shapes and then explain their layout and size choices based on the number of people living in the city. This project covers area, perimeter, and fractions, while also integrating maps and background knowledge of important buildings in a city, such as grocery stores, parks, pharmacies, gyms, homes, and restaurants. Another cross-curricular project may be to host a Socratic seminar about an illustration or photograph as it relates to the content being covered. For example, if you are discussing the Great Depression, you might present the photo "Migrant Mother" by Dorothea Lange and have students to respond to key questions. Then, during the seminar, listen as the conversation builds around the standard of living during the Great Depression. Afterward, students can write an explanation to answer how they would live on $12 per week to support their family based on standard cost of living estimates for food items.

An additional cross-curricular project could be an apocalypse project using Pablo Picasso's war painting, *Guernica*. To start the project, present the painting from Picasso while also explaining the context of the war effects in Europe. Next, present a timeline of key events relating to war and people's emotions during these times. The project would require students to create their own plan for surviving an apocalypse scenario, not unlike many of the war-ridden areas around the world. Students must include how they would feel in that situation, the materials they would use to survive, and how they would cope with their various emotions to survive the harsh living conditions. If students are open to the idea, they could include their own family histories and experiences in their project, while being sensitive to each other's backgrounds.

The last two projects are excellent opportunities for potentially gifted ELLs, as they require limited vocabulary through the usage of visual content, while also integrating higher order thinking, math, problem solving, and creative thinking skills. They also appeal to and support gifted ELLs who may have experienced hardships, such as poverty or harsh living conditions. When planning cross-curricular projects, consider the end goal, or what you want students to be able to do by the completion of the project. Also consider how the project supports heterogeneous learners at different academic and linguistic levels with higher order thinking skills and varying possible intelligences. Cross-curricular projects are an excellent method for developing and nurturing potential gifts and talents through student collaborative learning teams, problem solving, critical and creative thinking, and communication. Cross-curricular projects can also be especially beneficial for potentially gifted ELLs because they can include various forms of materials, such as illustrations, paintings, music, and animation, which can be accessed regardless of language proficiency.

Classroom teachers have the important and powerful role of juggling the needs of all of their students, including the needs of potentially gifted ELLs. The responsibility of the classroom teacher is multifaceted. They must (1) facilitate different activities and tasks to spark and ignite potential gifts and talents in ELLs, (2) recognize the potential gifts and talents of ELLs, and (3) continue to nurture these talents through extension and enrichment activities while also being cognizant of implicit bias regarding cultural norms. This is not an easy or simple responsibility. It demands ongoing support from the AIG teacher, the ELL teacher, parents, and administrators.

For ELL Teachers

The ELL teacher is also responsible for listening to and observing their students to recognize potential gifts and talents. However, most ELL teachers are not trained on what to look for and, in some cases, only have opportunities to work with struggling ELLs, leaving potentially gifted ELLs without language support or advocacy. This section explores five key steps for ELL teachers to help them spot indicators of giftedness when working with ELLs (see Figure 16).

Step 1: Start With Kindergarten. The most important first step is to begin early and start with kindergarten ELLs. Starting the process when students are younger gives them the necessary time for language development prior to gifted identification assessments. Additionally, starting at a younger age equips students with improved writing skills and vocabulary while fostering a safe learning environment for ELLs to

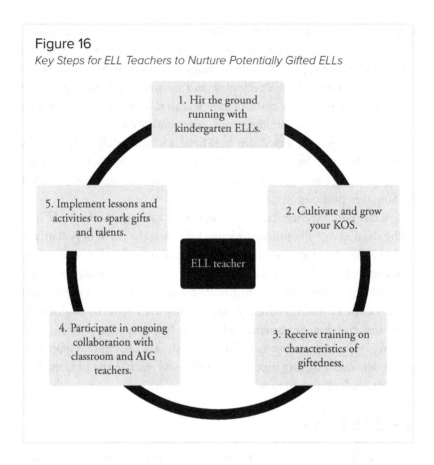

Figure 16
Key Steps for ELL Teachers to Nurture Potentially Gifted ELLs

develop free and creative thinking. If the ELL teacher waits until second grade or later to start supporting potentially gifted ELLs, the support may come too late, as most districts and states begin gifted program identification in second or third grade. This is why the ELL teacher is one of the foremost advocates for potentially gifted ELLs.

Step 2: Cultivate Your KOS. Because the ELL teacher has a particularly close working relationship with ELLs, lessons and activities lend themselves to be more individualized. ELL teachers are able to develop a greater depth of knowledge than classroom teachers because of the time that an ELL needs to become fully proficient in a language. Research indicates that becoming proficient in a new language, in all domains, takes 6–10 years. This translates to multiple years of ongoing language support from an ELL teacher in various settings, such as pull-out programs, push-in or coteaching models, or indirect instruction. This means that the ELL teacher is able to work with the same students for an extended amount of time if students are not transient, or moving from school to school. Some key details that an ELL teacher will want to learn include students' interests, academic background, pertinent information regarding parent communication and support, family culture, and students' hopes, dreams, and fears. The end goal is for the ELL teacher to have a clear understanding of all students to be able to plan lessons and activities to spark gifts and talents. Some ways that I have collected this information have included parent and student surveys, guiding students to create vision boards, creating a class culture quilt in which students created a patch to show their heritage, and hosting parent outreach events. Various activities and events such as these can bolster your knowledge of students and further the culture of advocacy for them. They can lead to observing students in settings outside of the classroom, such as birthday parties, dance performances, and sporting events. Ultimately, the goal is to develop a strong knowledge of your students from an early age to have as many opportunities as possible to spot potential talents and to foster a learning environment to nurture them.

Step 3: Receive Training on Gifted Characteristics. The observation step is also crucial. Looking and listening for potential talents involves using many data-collecting methods, such as conferring with students, listening to students during group sharing, observing students' work processes, analyzing students' completed work, and evaluating students' assessments or projects. But how do you know if what you are seeing and hearing is potentially gifted behavior? According to Renzulli (2005), there are three main characteristics that create the Three-Ring Conception of Giftedness: (1) above-average ability, (2) creativity, and (3) task commitment. Many researchers have listed numerous other identifiers of giftedness (and giftedness in ELLs); however, Renzulli's conception presents a simplified means for looking for potentially gifted ELLs. Using that criteria, I created a checklist that I consider when looking for potentially gifted ELLs (see Figure 17).

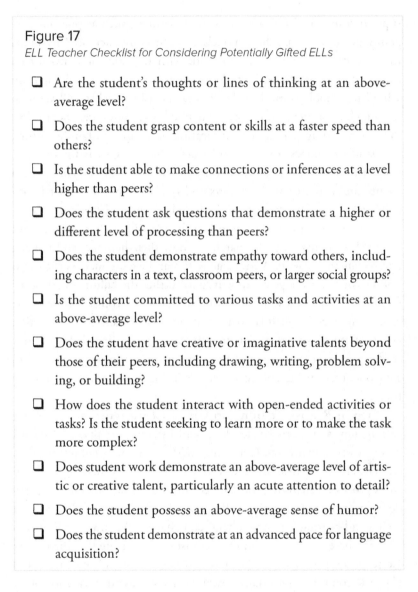

Figure 17
ELL Teacher Checklist for Considering Potentially Gifted ELLs

❏ Are the student's thoughts or lines of thinking at an above-average level?

❏ Does the student grasp content or skills at a faster speed than others?

❏ Is the student able to make connections or inferences at a level higher than peers?

❏ Does the student ask questions that demonstrate a higher or different level of processing than peers?

❏ Does the student demonstrate empathy toward others, including characters in a text, classroom peers, or larger social groups?

❏ Is the student committed to various tasks and activities at an above-average level?

❏ Does the student have creative or imaginative talents beyond those of their peers, including drawing, writing, problem solving, or building?

❏ How does the student interact with open-ended activities or tasks? Is the student seeking to learn more or to make the task more complex?

❏ Does student work demonstrate an above-average level of artistic or creative talent, particularly an acute attention to detail?

❏ Does the student possess an above-average sense of humor?

❏ Does the student demonstrate at an advanced pace for language acquisition?

A potentially gifted ELL does not need to meet all of these criteria, as all students are different and can possess varying degrees of academic and intellectual giftedness. Figure 17 presents questions to guide the ELL teacher's consideration of potentially gifted ELLs, but it does not encompass all forms of giftedness for potentially gifted ELLs. It is intended to serve as a point of consideration and possible conversation between the ELL and AIG teachers. Over the years, I have helped numerous ELLs to become identified as gifted ELLs, and all of them have demonstrated varying degrees of these behaviors. Some examples (with names changed for privacy) include:

- ▸ **Jewel:** This student was a young Vietnamese-American learner with great communication and verbal skills. She performed below grade level in reading and writing. I began working with her in second grade to develop her written expression and academic vocabulary. However, she didn't score enough points to qualify automatically for the gifted program. Jewel entered my radar for potential gifted behaviors because she qualified for a student portfolio to demonstrate possible gifts and talents. Over the year, Jewel worked with me and Melanie, the AIG teacher, to complete numerous tasks, including work samples for a student portfolio for gifted program consideration. Jewel consistently demonstrated a passion for learning and creating. Most students only complete the provided number of tasks for their portfolio, but Jewel completed multiple tasks. Jewel always wrote far beyond the minimum number of sentences, and she loved adding artistic details to her products. By the end of second grade, she was able to enroll in the district's gifted program as a gifted ELL.

- ▸ **Andy:** This student entered our school's ELL program as a kindergartner. He was the youngest boy in his family and entered school not knowing the letters or sounds of the alphabet. I began working with him in kindergarten but observed only grade-level or below-grade-level abilities. It wasn't until Andy entered first grade that I began to see potential gifts and talents, in large part due to his classroom teacher's high expectations from her students. Over the year, Andy went from performing far below grade level in reading to performing above grade level. Additionally, Andy demonstrated a unique line of thinking and creativity. When reading texts, he would draw conclusions about how certain characters must feel in the given situation, when most of his peers could not. Andy also asked questions about key details from a text that showed a higher level of thinking. Toward the end of first grade, students were asked to choose an illustration from *The Mysteries of Harris Burdick* by Chris Van Allsburg and create a story to explain the illustration. Andy created a complex and detailed creative story that was voted as the best story by the class. In second grade, Andy also entered into the gifted program.

▸ **Julio:** This student entered the ELL program in kindergarten and also demonstrated a below-average ability in reading comprehension. However, he demonstrated a faster-than-average pace for learning. He entered school knowing all of his letters and sounds but struggled with sight words and comprehension. Julio demonstrated a high need for tactile or sensory support. He hardly ever made eye contact with peers or teachers and repeatedly stomped his feet when walking in the hallway because he liked how it felt. Julio struggled with other social situations, as he had a sensitivity to loud noises and an obsessive fascination with tactile objects. Once, Julio wanted to use the sandbox to make word family words. But, instead of using the sandbox to build words, Julio poured the sand out of the sandbox onto the carpet because he liked the way it felt on his fingers. Julio's actions bothered the other kids who wanted to use the sandbox but now couldn't. Over the course of kindergarten, Julio exceeded expected growth to become an above-average reader. In first grade, he continued to demonstrate a faster rate of growth and above-average abilities in math, but he struggled with social skills. At one point in the year, he was asked to create a visual to teach a CVC, or consonant-vowel-consonant, word. He chose the word map and then created a drawing of a map that included battle ships, a landform with trees, sand, mountains, and a compass rose. His drawing was noteworthy compared to that of his peers because it continued from one side of the paper to the backside with continuous lines for the ocean and the land. It demonstrated a clear and strong understanding of perspective. Julio was flagged for potential giftedness for second grade by his first-grade teacher using the Gifted

Rating Scale, meaning that if he scored within a certain range in second grade, he would become eligible for the gifted program.

These students represent only some of the gifted behaviors that ELLs may exhibit. The purpose of sharing these students' learning histories is to showcase the varying types of giftedness you may observe. Alone, the students' behaviors do not indicate giftedness; it is the ELL teacher's holistic knowledge of the students, in collaboration with the AIG teacher's, that can lead these behaviors to be recognized as talents.

Step 4: Collaborate. Now that you have an idea of what to look for and you have observed some of these possible talents, it is time to discuss your observations with the AIG teacher and classroom teacher. Good conversations may start with explaining what you observed and then asking if the classroom teacher has observed similar things. The AIG teacher may offer more insight, based on your observations and guidance, to look for additional indicators. The purpose of this stage is to continue to advocate, so that all players are able to observe and nurture potential talents. It may be that the classroom teacher has not observed some of the same talents or behaviors that the ELL teacher has seen, so this would be a great opportunity to share and offer suggestions for possible classroom lessons or activities that would yield similar results. On the other hand, maybe you observed or made note of a student's response and want to ask the AIG teacher for clarification about if it could be considered above average. The key to this step is open and ongoing communication and collaboration between the ELL teacher, AIG teacher, and classroom teacher.

Step 5: Implement Lessons. The last step in this cyclical process is to create lessons and activities that can further spark potential gifts and talents, based on previous observations and your knowledge of students. These activities may include creative writing, STEM activities, projects, and many more. The next section will explore additional opportunities to spark potential gifts and talents. During these lessons and activities, you will actively observe students' work processes, lines of thinking, and end products. Your observations will be used to guide future instruction.

This is a cyclical process that is dependent on the ELL teacher's listening and observational data of students. It is also an ever-evolving process that is dependent on each step. The ELL teacher must have a strong knowledge of their students from as early as possible, a firm grasp on gifted indicators, and a collaborative team with which to discuss the needs of students to design meaningful lessons. During the lessons, the teacher should attune to students' work to make additional observations to gain insight into students' potential for giftedness, thereby guiding future lessons. If the ELL teacher is missing any one of the steps, this work becomes much more difficult. This is why the work of the previous chapters is crucial, prior to beginning the more complex work of identifying potentially gifted ELLs.

Possible Manifestations of Giftedness in Classroom Activities

"I don't work at being ordinary."

—Paul McCartney

As important as it is to be knowledgeable about the various intelligences and methods of observing for potential gifts and talent, it is just as important to know how to recognize potential gifts in your own classroom. This next section explores what the various forms of intelligence may look like in the classroom, as well as examples of various lessons and activities. Some of the examples also include what an end product may look like by a potentially gifted student. The purpose of this section is to present an array of forms that giftedness may take in a classroom setting to educate and inspire teachers for future lesson selections.

For Teachers and Administrators

Multiple Intelligences in the Classroom. Multiple intelligences (Gardner 1983/2011) in the classroom are not stressed nearly as much as they should be because of the testing environment in most school programs. Sadly, this environment fosters the incorrect assumption that test results correlate to retained information. Yet, some of the most impactful artists and figures throughout history exhibited forms of multiple intelligences. Examples of artists with multiple intelligences include Paul McCartney, Aretha Franklin, John Williams, Stevie Wonder, and Madonna. These artists were able to write or compose their own music and perform at a level far above others in the industry by creating multiple musical works time and time again. These artists consistently integrated creativity, strong emotions, imagination, motivation, and other indicators of giftedness.

If teachers listen for multiple intelligences in the classroom, what would they look or sound like? Table 4 explains what these gifts and talents may look like in different areas.

As noted previously, these intelligences may be viewed through cross-curricular projects, project-based learning, and student learning teams. Gifted students' end products will have the same components as their peers, but they will also have additional components beyond those of their classmates. In the Flat Stanley project, a gifted student's visual of Stanley may include more attention to artistic detail, such as color choice and coloring precision. Gifted students also may go beyond collecting the pictures and, instead, create a photo album or scrapbook of Flat Stanley's travelling adventures. In this example the teacher should not set too many requirements on the end product, because this can stifle student creativity. Rather, it is better to have a clear rubric for content expectations so that potentially gifted students may have opportunities to show their critical and creative thinking skills. In the geometric city example, a gifted student may take on a leadership role to offer mathematical support or guidance on map layouts. The student may also want to make the city layout complex or detailed by including buildings or sites that may seem unimportant to peers, such as ponds within the park or a small post office drop box outside of the larger post office building. Additionally, they may seek to make the geometric rendering of the city as near to perfect as possible, with fractional representations of buildings.

The Socratic seminar project and the apocalypse project offer especially good opportunities for gifted ELLs to demonstrate their abilities because they require minimal academic vocabulary. Within the seminar project, students may be particularly insightful and empathetic in their

Table 4

Manifestations of Giftedness Using Multiple Intelligence Theory

Areas of Giftedness	Manifestations
Academic	▶ Strong academic language knowledge. ▶ Ability to clearly express themselves, potentially in more than one language. ▶ Rapid pace of learning new skills.
Attention and motivation	▶ Strong attention to detail, including drawings and performances. ▶ Ability to focus or have "tunnel vision" with tasks that are pertinent or of interest to the student for extended periods of time.
Creativity and the arts	▶ Unique ability to represent ideas and concepts in visuals, performances, or products. ▶ Can clearly create works of art or forms of expression far above peers.
Curiosity	▶ Possess a unique curiosity about the "why" behind concepts that may seem mundane to peers, or philosophical to an adult.
Humor	▶ Easily understand jokes, puns, or witty phrases. ▶ Can create their own play on words or jokes.
Imagination	▶ Possess an exceptional imagination for interpreting or reimagining content in new ways. ▶ Can clearly visualize images and/or details in their head but may struggle to express them without practice.
Perspective	▶ Pose unique questions that most peers would not consider. ▶ Can explore and empathize with different points of view outside of their own.
Problem solving	▶ Enjoy solving problems using multistep processes to get to the bottom of a problem.
Social challenges and emotional intensity	▶ Easily frustrated with others who may not grasp skills as quickly or who don't understand their perspective. ▶ Wide and deep range of emotions, including empathy toward others and sensitivity to inequities and social injustice.

responses during the discussion. They may also ask pertinent questions to gain a greater understanding of how challenging life was during this time in history. After the discussion, gifted learners may create a detailed and mathematically sound method for surviving, on a limited budget, within a stressful situation that others may not have considered. For the apocalypse project, gifted students may demonstrate a strong sense of empathy toward victims. They may also recognize the symbolism and attention to detail within Picasso's painting that they may, in turn, struggle to express to peers. The gifted students' plans for surviving may also be very detailed and complex, including considering humanitarian needs that their peers have not considered, such as insulating or fortifying shelters for security or to protect themselves from the elements. One of the most important aspects of cross-curricular projects is the offering of many opportunities for students to demonstrate their varied talents, such as leadership, problem solving, imagination, and creativity. Teachers should not offer exemplars because they may stifle creativity. Instead teachers are encouraged to provide students with detailed rubrics and incorporate time to confer with students or learning teams to pose critical thinking questions regarding their end product. Conferring with students allows the teacher to support students with feedback and questions. An example of conferring that may take place during the apocalypse project may look like this:

Teacher: I see that you have considered food, water, and shelter in making your survival plan. How will you make sure that your food and water are safe to consume?

Student: I will find packaged food and bottled water.

Teacher: What happens if you cannot find bottled water?

Student: I will go to a creek or a river.

Teacher: How will you make sure that water is safe to drink?

Student: Hmm . . . I am not sure. I will look it up to
                    make a new plan.

This example highlights how the teacher can guide the student to a higher level of thinking without presenting the end question first, helping the student to expand their learning in ways that they may not have considered.

With varying types of giftedness, the culture of advocacy must extend beyond the ELL, AIG, and classroom teachers. Additional school staff can listen and observe gifts and talents, across multiple subjects and in various settings. Teacher assistants, as well as teachers of the arts (e.g., music, dance, and visual art teachers), are also able to observe potential gifts and talents but must be trained on what to look for when working with ELLs. By training all staff members, and creating a strong culture of advocacy, more students can be considered for gifted programs.

Lessons and Activities to Spark Gifts and Talents. Like parents, teachers want to make sure that they are doing the right thing for children, but they are not always sure what that is. However, data always act as a clear and indisputable guide. Table 5 outlines assignments that teachers of gifted learners carried out, along with the activity outcomes (Kitano & Pedersen, 2002).

According to Kitano and Pedersen (2002), gifted ELLs show greater independence than typical ELLs, prefer a faster pace, and prefer challenge to remedial instruction. Table 6 presents additional activities that integrate student independence and ability to pace their own learning. These activities are intended to spark creative thinking and allow teachers and parents to see possible indicators of giftedness, along with the corresponding product that a gifted learner may produce for that activity.

These tasks are great activities to discover gifts and talents in the classroom because they are manageable for the teacher, and they integrate multiple methods for potentially gifted students to demonstrate talents. They are especially excellent activities because they require minimal academic vocabulary, thus providing potentially gifted ELLs with equal opportunity to demonstrate giftedness without language constraints. Additionally, many of the activities support content standards

Table 5

Sample Activities From AIG Teachers (Kitano & Pedersen, 2002)

Grade Level	Assignment Description	Activity Outcome
3	Select a biography to read based on your interests.	After reading about their person of choice, students chose to create posters about their researched subject. They also chose to dress up like their subjects and give a presentation in the voice of those subjects, similar to a living museum experience, but this example was student led.
3 and 4 combined	Read biographies of composers and visual artists.	The teacher played the music of a preselected composer and shared various examples of artwork. Students then chose to design and create a student-led project from this information. They used the information gleaned from the music and art to create a timeline of artists' work that included historical events of the time period. This activity activated students' background knowledge and interests to connect with the current content to create a method for organizing or sorting their knowledge through the use of a timeline.
6	Within small groups, research different civilizations, such as Ancient Egypt.	The class chose to turn the assignment into their own student-led research project by brainstorming categories of knowledge to research on their various civilizations. They collectively decided on 11 key topics of a civilization, such as clothing, writing, technologies, and games. The small groups then researched their civilization in depth to identify the 11 key topics for their area and created a display for families and the school to see their understanding.
Unknown	Research and learn about George Washington.	The teacher provided multiple biographies on George Washington at various reading levels for the students to choose their own text that they found to be the most interesting to them. This is a good example of student choice and a student-driven lesson within academic learning.

Table 6
Activities to Ignite Talent With Corresponding Possible Manifestations

Activity	Type	Corresponding Grade Level	Activity Description	A Gifted ELL's Product May Look Like . . .
Fruity Tooty	Creative thinking, verbal reasoning, and supporting opinions	K–2	Pose the following question to students and have them create a visual to support their verbal response: What kind of fruit would you be, and why?	A well-articulated and original response to the fruit that most closely matches their personality. It may include a rare fruit or a particularly clear description for why that fruit matches them best.
Imagination Squiggle	Creative thinking and problem solving	K–2	Present students with a Squiggle Sheet. Explain that they will create something new and different using the squiggle on their sheet. You may choose to front-load this activity by reading the book *Beautiful Oops!* by Barney Saltzberg.	A vivid rendering of their "something new" for their squiggle. It may be a very unique interpretation of the squiggle, or it may exhibit a close attention to detail, such as color choice or attentiveness to details. For example, they may have turned the squiggle into a leaf, drew the veins on the leaf, and then drew a tree with clear shades of bark connecting to that leaf.

Table 6, *continued*

Activity	Type	Corresponding Grade Level	Activity Description	A Gifted ELL's Product May Look Like . . .
Mission: World Peace	Explain ideas, recall facts, and support opinion using verbal reasoning	K–4	Pose the following question to students and have them create a visual to support their verbal response: How would you make the people of the world all get along?	A strong opinion of how they plan to make the world better. It may include personal beliefs of what is right or just, along with equally strong beliefs of what is wrong and how to fix these social inequities. Their visual may include detail-specific examples of their plan with key members or key areas of society that need improvement. Their visual may contain a wider use of color or detail in their drawing.
Animal, Schmanimal	Creative thinking, problem solving, critical thinking, and evaluation	1–3	Pose the following task to students: *Choose 2–3 animals that you would like to combine to create a new and original animal. Create a drawing of your new animal and explain what makes this new animal unique.*	A creative visual of a new animal. Their drawing may include rare or uncommon animal choices than those of their peers, and it may include unique abilities. It will also include a fine attention to details.

Table 6, *continued*

Activity	Type	Corresponding Grade Level	Activity Description	A Gifted ELL's Product May Look Like . . .
Math Machine	Problem solving, critical thinking, and verbal expression	1–5	Ask students to create a math problem-solving machine visual. It can be a machine to solve any type of math problem, but it must follow a specific rule that is the same for every math problem. The student must explain how the machine works and give examples of problems it can solve.	A clear and well-organized visual that shows a strong understanding of mathematical rules and problem solving. Their machine may include a higher level of complexity or multistep problem solving. Their example problems may also be more challenging than those of peers, as they may require a multistep solution.
Island Simulation	Explain ideas and opinions in a new situation, provide evidence, and support opinion using reasoning	2–5	Pose the following question to students and have them create a multistep visual, including a map to support their verbal response: You are alone on an island. What do you do next?	A well-organized multistep rendering of their process to explore and successfully navigate around the island. It may include important resources, such as fresh water, safe living area, and sources for food, and it should demonstrate an understanding of map reading, such as a compass rose or land features like mountains, rivers, etc. Their visual may include strong attention to detail, such as with color selection or spatial awareness (e.g., a tree is drawn smaller than a mountain, or a fruit is drawn smaller than a river).

Table 6, *continued*

Activity	Type	Corresponding Grade Level	Activity Description	A Gifted ELLs Product May Look Like . . .
Invention, Invention, What's Your Deduction?	Critical thinking, evaluation, and application of knowledge	2–7	Pose the following question to students and have them create a visual to support their verbal response: What invention do you think has helped society the most? Why?	A clear and well-organized argument to explain the best invention for society, including key details and reasons. Their response may include more details, key vocabulary, or information compared to that of peers. Their visual may also include more attention to details, such as color or physical features of that invention.
Project Carnival or Project Casino	Problem solving, creative thinking, critical thinking, and application	2 and up	Present the following project for students to complete: Create a carnival/casino game that is mathematically rigged in your favor but is not blatantly obvious to the players of the game. Example games could include a ring toss or slot machines. Student projects should be fun and engaging. They must include: ▶ Rules/directions for playing the game. ▶ Monetary price for playing the game.	A fun and engaging game that is especially challenging for players to win while not obvious to the player. It may demonstrate a wide and varied range of mathematical knowledge. There should be a strong understanding of probability demonstrated in their end product.

Table 6, *continued*

Activity	Type	Corresponding Grade Level	Activity Description	A Gifted ELL's Product May Look Like . . .
Project Carnival or Project Casino, *continued*			▸ Monetary prize for winning the grand prize, along with mathematical odds for winning the grand prize that can be shared after players play their game. ▸ Profit margin for the House (e.g., for every five players, one player wins, so if the game cost $1 to play, the house makes $4 dollars for every $1 lost).	
Tweet Tweet, Let Them Speak	Creative thinking and application of knowledge	2 and up	Ask students to do the following: Create a tweet in the voice of your favorite book character. An example tweet from Hermione might be: "So many books to read and so little time for this summer vacation. Looking forward to using my new watch #thanksprofDumbledore #litesummerreading #magicmastery"	A vivid representation of that character's thinking/perspective. It may include content-specific vocabulary, creative wordplay/puns, or a unique sense of humor.

Table 6, *continued*

Activity	Type	Corresponding Grade Level	Activity Description	A Gifted ELLs Product May Look Like . . .
Mentor Inquisition	Critical thinking and verbal reasoning	4 and up	Pose the following question to students and have them create a verbal and/or written response with supporting evidence: Who would you choose to be your mentor from the past, and why?	A clear and well-organized argument to choose their role model/mentor, including key details and reasons. Their response may include more details, key vocabulary, or information compared to that of peers.
Musical Ingenuity	Creative thinking and application of knowledge	4 and up	Ask students to write a song in the voice of their favorite singer (e.g., Justin Timberlake, Taylor Swift, or Kanye West).	A clear attention to detail in the voice of their singer or in word choice. It may incorporate humor or vivid imagery from the perspective of that singer.
Mock Trial	Apply knowledge of key details and argue a point with clear deductive reasoning skills	6 and up	Divide your class into the following groups: 4–8 lawyers (half for the defense and half for the prosecution) and 4–6 key witnesses. The remaining students will be the jury, while you, the teacher, will serve as the judge. Assign students roles based on the content area, and then facilitate time for research to prepare for the trial. Then allow for 2–4 days for the actual trial.	Clear attention to detail for their role within the mock trial, including the "voice" of their role, traits of that role, and a strong ability to act/impersonate that role. Gifted ELLs may benefit from serving as a lawyer to develop their verbal expressive skills while also showing their strong attention to detail, argumentative skills, and reasoning skills.

and can be easily integrated into unit plans for students to demonstrate mastery.

Professional Development for Parents, Teachers, and Students

After considering the indicators of giftedness and what giftedness may look like in various cultures and academic settings, it is important to revisit perception. Regardless of adults' open-mindedness, ELLs still face many challenges to becoming identified and supported in gifted programs. This section provides an activity for parents, teachers, and students to guide their reflections about what giftedness may look like. More often than not, children are not considered for gifted programs due to bias, even when teachers are seeking to make a necessary mind shift toward dynamic thinking about underrepresented populations. The following activity introduces immigrants who have made impressive impacts on society. It can be used with students in grades 1–12 depending on the goal of the activity, at parent outreach events, at professional development trainings for teachers, or to guide state and district leaders. The activity deals with reading comprehension, biographies, history, science, and multiple higher order thinking skills to introduce immigrants from various backgrounds. The purpose of this activity is to help participants to reflect upon who can be gifted and what giftedness may look or sound like.

Inspiring, Impressive, and Impactful Immigrants (I4) Activity. The activity leader (AL) will put participants into learning teams (LTs) of about 3–6 people per team. Next, the AL will provide LTs with a case study of a gifted immigrant from the task cards in Figure 18. The LTs will read their task card and discuss their case subject. Next, the AL will provide LTs with an anchor chart or blank poster. LTs will synthesize the key details about this gifted immigrant to create a graffiti poster; multiple individuals take notes through visuals on a single poster. Their graffiti poster may include words but should mostly tell a story or portray information through visuals. After LTs have completed their posters, they will hang up their graffiti posters around the room. LTs will then complete a gallery walk, during which they will walk to different posters

Figure 18

Inspiring, Impressive, and Impactful Immigrants (I4) Task Cards

I was born March 3, 1847, in Edinburg, Scotland. My father specialized in the art of public speaking, specifically voice and elocution. My mother struggled with hearing but later became a great pianist. Later in life, I taught deaf people to communicate using the placement of their tongue and lips to form visibly recognizable words. I continued to study the parts of sound by analyzing the vibrations or resonance of the mouth to speak. In 1871, I immigrated to the United States where I continued to support the deaf at the world's first school for the deaf. My passion for studying sound and helping the deaf to hear led to my most notable invention in 1876. I invented the telephone.

Who am I?

I am Alexander Graham Bell.

I was born July 10, 1856, in Smiljan, Croatia. I grew up very poor. My father was an orthodox priest, and my mother was not educated. I was sick a lot as a child and was homeschooled. Later, I attended school and enjoyed poetry. I also had a creative imagination and photographic memory. Some of my teachers thought that I cheated at math because I could solve integral calculus in my mind. In 1884, I moved to the United States with only 4 cents in my pocket. I later went on to invent the first alternating current (AC) motor, AC generation, and transmission technology. I made large contributions in the area of electricity that are still used today.

Who am I?

I am Nikola Tesla.

Figure 18, *continued*

I was born June 28, 1971, in Pretoria, South Africa. I loved to read, especially comic books. Due to my quick remarks, teachers and adults would call me a smart aleck. I attended an English-speaking preparatory school where I was bullied a lot as a child by other kids because I was smarter than most. At age 10, I started building my own videogame, and at age 12, I sold the game to Spectravideo for $500. In 1992, I moved to the U.S. after studying in Canada for a few years. I went on to get a bachelor's degree in physics and economics. I have helped to create companies such as Zip2, PayPal, and SolarCity. I am most well-known for creating the Tesla car models that do not require oil to run and for my SpaceX business.

Who am I?

I am Elon Musk.

I was born February 11, 1847, in Milan, OH. Both of my parents were immigrants before they moved to Ohio. I had a case of scarlet fever as a child and numerous ear infections that caused several hearing problems that turned into deafness as an adult. Because I could not hear very well in school, teachers thought that I was not very intelligent. I was hyperactive in the classroom; teachers believed I had behavior problems. I had an above-average-sized forehead, making me a target for bullying from peers. After only a short period of time in school, my mom chose to homeschool me because of concerns from teachers. I later created several notable inventions to become known as one of the greatest inventors of all time. Some of those inventions include the phonograph, the electrical light bulb, and silent movies.

Who am I?

I am Thomas Edison.

Figure 18, *continued*

I was born March 14, 1879, in Württemberg, Germany. It took me longer than normal to learn how to talk. I didn't start talking until 3 or 4 years old. Contrary to popular belief, I never failed in mathematics. I hated my primary school experience because it wasn't open to questioning, creative thinking, or original thought. At age 16, I ran away from boarding school, but later my parents still made me take my exams. I excelled in math and physics classes but failed French, chemistry, and biology. In 1902, I was fired from multiple jobs trying to tutor children and struggled to make any money. The same year my father died thinking I was failure. Soon after, I became employed, pursued my doctorate, and entered the field of academic research. I moved to the America in 1932 and became a U.S. citizen in 1940. I am most well-known for my theory of relativity, contributions to the field of physics, and receiving a Nobel Peace Prize.

Who am I?

I am Albert Einstein.

I was born August 27, 1942, in Communist China. My original name was Yee Ching Wong, but my parents later helped me to change it to be more English friendly. For primary school, I attended an all-girl Catholic school in Hong Kong, China, where I excelled in math and science. I was a good, hard-working student. I did not enjoy learning about the sciences, but my parents encouraged me to learn more about them. No women in my family had ever worked outside of the home. In 1965, I moved to the U.S. to begin my studies as a bachelor student in Los Angeles, CA. After several years of coursework, I earned my bachelor's in bacteriology and my Ph.D. in molecular biology. In 1985, I was the first researcher to clone HIV, which has helped doctors to better understand the genetics of the virus as well as the development of blood tests. In 2007, I was named as one of the "Top 100 Living Geniuses" according to *The Daily Telegraph*.

Who am I?

I am Flossie Wong-Staal.

Note. Task card biographical information was gathered from Encyclopedia of World Biography (n.d.), Gregersen (2020), History.com editors (2020), Isaacson (2007), Josephson (2020), Kaku (n.d.), and PBS (n.d.).

with sticky notes and pens. Once at a team's poster, the LT will read the graffiti. As a group, they will discuss the individual on the poster to answer the following targeted key questions:

- ▶ For students:
  - ▹ How are you similar to these inspiring, impressive, and impactful immigrants?
  - ▹ How are you different from these impressive and impactful immigrants?

- ▶ For teachers:
  - ▹ What gifted behaviors can you observe in these case studies?
  - ▹ Would you have recognized these gifted talents from this inspiring, impressive, and impactful immigrant if they were in your class today?

- ▶ For parents:
  - ▹ What role did parents play in supporting these impressive and impactful immigrants?
  - ▹ What gifted behaviors can you observe in these case studies?

LTs will record their group answers to the questions on their sticky note and attach it to the graffiti poster for that individual. Each LT should put one sticky note on each poster. LTs will continue rotating to the different posters until all teams have added a note with their responses on each poster. Afterward, LTs will return to their original graffiti poster and read other teams' responses to identify the most common answers for their questions. Next, the AL will guide the LTs to share out the consensus answers for that poster. Finally, the AL will have LTs return to their seats. The AL will pose several reflective questions for activity participants to discuss with their team and then share out:

- ▶ What was the purpose of this activity?
- ▶ Why do you think some immigrants would have been identified as gifted, while others would not have been?
- ▶ Did your understanding of what giftedness can look like change in this activity? How?
- ▶ How does this activity impact your understanding of giftedness?

Ultimately, the purpose of this activity is to provide students with examples of immigrant role models and to show students that giftedness has many forms. Offering students examples of gifted immigrants can help to ignite and inspire gifted ELLs to achieve similar greatness in the future, as well as show classroom teachers the dangers of first impressions of culturally diverse students, particularly with the case study of Thomas Edison. This activity can also be used to teach parents about the importance of their roles to shape and nurture their children's gifts and talents. By learning about others' experiences in school, they can learn how to support their own ELLs.

Chapter Summary

Listening is a simple enough skill in concept, but it is also quite complex because of its openness to interpretation and analysis. How many times have you had a conversation with someone, only to replay that same conversation in your head later on to fully understand what was said? Listening and observing to nurture potentially gifted ELLs' talents is a crucial step in the process to identify students in underrepresented populations in gifted programs. It not only relies on key players to be knowledgeable about the indicators of giftedness, but also depends on their ability to provide opportunities to look for gifted behaviors. Most importantly, it relies on key players' abilities to interpret and understand what they hear and observe from potentially gifted students.

This chapter presented parents with a list of indicators of giftedness, as well as what gifted behaviors may look like in a classroom. It showed the importance of the ELL teacher to be able to recognize, nurture, and advocate for potentially gifted ELLs. For teachers, it explained what giftedness may look like for culturally diverse students, and it explained the importance of considering multiple intelligences when planning lessons. This chapter explained how teachers can use cross-curricular activities to spark gifts and talents and what products from those activities may look like for gifted ELLs. Finally, it culminated with an activity to help students, teachers, and parents to better understand the forms that giftedness may take. So how can students come to be identified and enrolled in gifted programs? This will be explored in the following chapter.

Discussion Questions

1. What are some of the indicators of giftedness?
2. How do these indicators vary in students with CLED backgrounds?
3. How can gifted behaviors appear differently in students' work?
4. What is your plan to ignite potential gifts and talents in learners, and how will you listen or observe for these talents?

CHAPTER 4

Act

Putting Action Behind Ideas and Research to Identify Gifted ELLs

> "There are risks and costs to action. But they are far less than the long-range risks of comfortable inaction."
>
> —John F. Kennedy

Now that you are equipped to see possible gifts and talents in different areas, how do you nurture them to grow into something more? This section explores how key players can nurture gifts and talents in the classroom, based on previous observations. Up to this point, you have learned about creating collaborative teams within the school to support potentially gifted ELLs, extending the culture of advocacy within the school, and developing a strong knowledge of your students and the indicators of giftedness. All of these are crucial for nurturing potential talents of gifted children. This next stage builds upon that work to nurture gifts and talents and to support potentially gifted ELLs through the identification process. Much like the collaborative team in the school, the work of identifying gifted children varies from district to district and state to state. This section seeks to provide an overview of programs that have been successful in increasing identified CLED students for gifted programs. It also proposes next steps for key players based on the most relevant research on identifying gifted ELLs.

Nurturing Gifts and Talents: For Administrators and Teachers

According to Merriam-Webster, the act of nurturing is the sum of the environmental factors influencing the behaviors and traits expressed by an organism. The term *nurture* is often used to refer to helping plants grow to their fullest potential. In the case of a plant, those environmental factors include sunlight exposure, sunlight duration, watering frequency and quantity, and protection from human or animal interference. For the purposes of this book, nurturing gifts and talents requires the consideration of multiple environmental factors, such as when the student is at school and when the student is outside of school. This section explores the ideal environmental factors to nurture gifts and talents in ELLs in the classroom.

The Ideal Gifted ELL Classroom

There are multiple factors that can help to nurture the gifts and talents of ELLs to help them grow in the classroom setting. There are also multiple factors that can prevent the gifts and talents of ELLs from getting support, leaving those talents to wither. Therefore, it is the responsibility of the ELL teacher, AIG teacher, and classroom teacher to construct as many ideal situational factors as possible from the comprehensive list in Table 7.

This comprehensive list integrates the best teaching practices and strategies that research has to offer. The list may seem daunting and overwhelming, especially for newer teachers. Therefore, it is suggested to select a small number of areas that you would like to target in an outlined amount of time. A newer teacher may choose to tackle one or two areas, while a veteran teacher may recognize that they already implement several practices and would like to improve in one or two areas. In terms of gifted ELLs, it is better to have a few well-grown

Table 7

*Traditional Classroom Compared to Ideal
Learning Environment for Gifted ELLs*

Traditional Classroom	Ideal Learning Environment for Gifted ELLs
Limited seating options.	Flexible seating options for various learning styles.
Requires students to acclimate to dominant cultural norms (e.g., requires eye contact, asks students to stop being shy, ignores students' backgrounds, etc.).	Teacher embraces students' interests, cultures, and backgrounds.
Teacher only advocates for low-achieving students and ignores high-achieving students.	Teacher creates a culture of advocacy for all students.
All students complete the same tasks at the same level of difficulty.	Students complete differentiated tasks based on their individual needs.
Makes excuses for students who do not meet expectations.	Sets high expectations for all students and supports all students to reach them.
Provides feedback in grading assignments but misses feedback to support students' growth in areas of need.	Provides meaningful feedback to students to guide their learning.
Standard-driven content.	Student-driven content; students choose what they want to learn more about.
Teacher led.	Student led.
Teacher has limited knowledge of students (only academic knowledge; missing student personalities, interests, culture, and family dynamic).	Teacher has an in-depth and evolving knowledge of students' lives and interests.

Table 7, *continued*

Traditional Classroom	Ideal Learning Environment for Gifted ELLs
Lessons and units include exit and end goal expectations but are missing the purpose behind this end goal.	Lessons and units have a clear end goal of what mastery will look like based on language proficiency knowledge and purpose of the lesson.
Tasks and lessons may include relevancy but do not provide meaning or purpose for students.	Tasks and lessons explain relevancy and purpose to give all students buy-in to the lesson.
Incorporates writing occasionally, but only to show comprehension of a text with text-dependent questions.	Incorporates creative writing opportunities for students to develop their imagination and problem-solving skills.
Students have 1–2 opportunities for learning (whole-class instruction or independent practice).	Students have multiple opportunities to grapple with content (station teaching, centers, learning teams, teacher conferring, etc.).
One method or form to show mastery (e.g., a test).	Offers multiple methods to show mastery (e.g., projects, performances, displays, etc.).
Learning is very easy for some and very challenging for others.	Learning is challenging for all because of differentiated tasks based on students' individual needs.
Ignores social and emotional needs of students who are different.	Embraces and supports students' social and emotional needs through bibliotherapy.
Teacher reflects upon their teaching practices for future lessons.	Teacher reflects upon their own practices as well as guides students to reflect upon their learning.
Teacher sets learning goals for students based on norm-referenced data.	Teacher guides students to create their own learning goals through conferring based on individual feedback.

Table 7, *continued*

Traditional Classroom	Ideal Learning Environment for Gifted ELLs
Limited learning autonomy for students; the teacher selects the content and pace.	Students are responsible for their learning and pace for learning.
Low level of student engagement and student motivation.	High level of student engagement and motivation for learning.
Incorporates worksheets and lower level thinking according to Bloom's taxonomy to show understanding.	Incorporates choice boards, contracts, project-based learning opportunities, and learning pathways.
The teacher is doing most of the work.	Students are doing the majority of the work.

plants than several plants that are withering. In other words, it is better to implement one factor very well than to work on several areas poorly.

Establishing Routines and Gradual Release to Build Independent Learners

Continuing to differentiate is one meaningful method for teaching identified gifted ELLs. Once you have created a handful of differentiated activities and tasks for a concept, you can begin the process of gradual release to create independent learners. This is important not just for gifted ELLs, but for all students. For students to learn a skill, they must be able to practice that skill or concept multiple times. Teaching new activities or tasks requires this same approach so that students can become responsible for their own learning. Figure 19 shows how to carry out each phase of the gradual release process.

Gradual release begins with you, the teacher, teaching one task or activity for the day. After teaching all of the steps needed for this task, including a solution station where students can visit for help without bringing their work to copy, students turn and tell their partner how to do this activity/task. Telling a partner how to do this activity builds

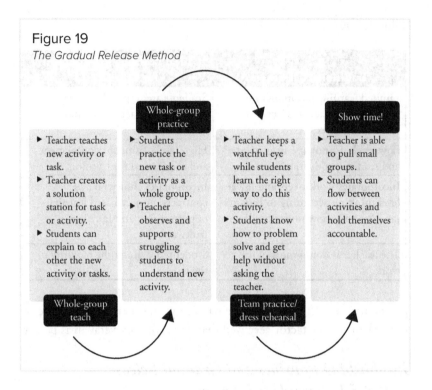

Figure 19
The Gradual Release Method

academic language, ensures that students are listening to directions, encourages students to remember the steps, and allows struggling learners to hear the task for a second time. Once students have told their partner, you will lead the entire class to practice the task/activity. You can differentiate the content or the question difficulty of the activity or task, but by making the steps the same for everyone, teaching the task becomes easier. You can also change content without having to teach a whole new task.

For example, using a task called Infinite Writing Ideas, students can choose a writing prompt to create an imaginative and unique writing piece. The writing prompts are varied, based on students' written skills, but all students complete the same steps for creating, editing, and publishing their writing task. As the year goes on, you can use new writing prompts and not have to reteach the whole activity. As students practice the new task/activity as a whole group, you must walk around to ensure that students know what to do, how to do it, and how to get help. You will also need to address any negative behaviors, such as off-task students wandering around the room or complacent sitters—those students who wait to be spoon-fed. To correct the off-task student, you may encourage students to ask a friend to repeat the directions or immediately positively reinforce the behaviors of those who are on task. For example, if Jose is off-task while Camila is doing a great job, the teacher would take a moment to recognize Camila by saying, "Wow! Camila, I love how you are using your resources to work out that problem." This shows Jose that he can use resources, too, without embarrassing him in front of others. Students who are wandering the classroom will need to be reminded of station expectations, including where materials are located and how to problem solve. If multiple students are off-task, it may be time to have a reflection.

Students who are waiting to be spoon-fed may need additional positive reinforcement as they complete more simple steps to boost their self-esteem and self-confidence. They may be scared to mess up or fail. By recognizing positive accomplishments, you will help them to believe in their own abilities. An example of supportive reinforcement for writing may take place after students write their introduction or create a detailed graphic organizer. This would be an ideal time to recognize their accomplishment, as well as to help them reflect on how they reached that step and what the next step should be. Helping students to celebrate and reflect upon their abilities helps them to realize that they can be independent learners and reverse negative self-esteem.

To wrap up the first day of teaching a new task/activity, you will need to have a reflection meeting. I usually have my students sit in a circle to share what went well during our practice and what we need to keep working on. This supports students who struggle to remember what to do the next time. Students may share about how everyone got to practice the skill, how some people knew how to use the solution station, and how a few students helped show others what to do. Students may also share that too many people were wandering around the classroom or that the noise level was too loud for others to focus. You will want to guide this reflection to ask what should be worked on next time to make this activity time better. For instance, students may say they need to work on making sure everyone knows where to find resources. The next day, before teaching a new task or activity, you can ask students to review the station from the day before, including what they need to work on for the day. This helps students to remember the previous task before adding on a new task.

As you teach a new task, repeat the steps for it, including teacher modeling, student turn and talk, and student practice. You will continue this process of reviewing, teaching, and practicing tasks until students know what to do for every activity, how to do it, and how to get help. Once the tasks/activities have been taught, host a few days of team practice. This is when students form learning teams to choose which task or activity they wish to complete. I allow my students to choose their own station and how long they wish to stay there. This is possible because I have a clear rubric for every station, including the end goal of each station, such as a solution or an exemplar. Students must recognize the importance of quality over quantity. I require students to publish one of their creative works each month, so that they are not just writing one sentence and then rushing to another station. This helps to build student choice and accountability. It also teaches students to drive their own learning by focusing on the written piece that matters the most to them.

While student learning teams are practicing whichever task they choose, actively observe the students, so that they know they are being watched and will be inclined to do the right things. This shows students that you care about their work and their product; if students think you do not care or are only giving them busy work, then they do not care about the end product either. Additionally, as you are actively observing the classroom, address any negative behaviors. If more than one third of the class is off-task or unable to work in learning teams, end the activity time early to move into a reflection circle. You will never want to keep activity time going if more than a third of the class is off-task; this would reinforce negative behaviors and lead to other students becoming off-task as well.

After teaching the activities, setting up routines, and teaching the reflection circle, it is time for the "dress rehearsal" activity time. The purpose of this time is to ensure that all students can complete the tasks/activities without the teacher, supporting independent learning and grapple time. I usually have dress rehearsal activity practice for 1–3 days, or possibly a whole week for younger students. After every dress rehearsal, remember to host a reflective circle share to continue reinforcing positive behaviors and correcting any negative behaviors as a class. Eventually, after several days of team practice using the dress rehearsal time, in which the teacher actively observes the students working, the class will be ready for "show time."

The final stage of gradual release is show time, when all students work at their own pace, and at their own level on any chosen activity or task while the teacher can begin working with groups or conferring with students. At this time, some teachers may use a visual to show younger students that they cannot interrupt the teacher, such as a glow stick necklace, a push-on light, or a silly hat; if the teacher is wearing or using said item, it means that it is show time, and students cannot interrupt. At this stage, teachers will still need to keep a watchful eye to ensure all students are engaged and guide students to reflect during circle share about what went well and what some areas for continued growth may be. This continuous reflection time is crucial, not only for behaviors, but also for learning and developing verbal skills.

Once students are in tune with the behavioral expectations of activity time, circle share may move to include students answering questions about how they were challenged and how what they learned can help them in the future. Teachers are encouraged to create a routine for this activity time, including using a visual timer for students to self-monitor, teaching clear expectations for cleanup, and guiding students to lead the circle reflection share.

After my students have mastered gradual release, I transition them to partner share how they grew as a learner by choosing a reflection question from an anchor chart. Some of my reflection questions include:

- How did you grow as a learner?
- How can you use what you learned today?
- What was challenging about the task today?
- What are your next steps to advance your knowledge in this area?

By having students share with their partner the answer to one of these reflective questions, they are able to remember what they learned and bolster their academic verbal skills.

Sample Activity

For students to make choices about their learning that are based on their own understanding of their talents and abilities, teachers must have a strong knowledge of their students, including potential areas of talent. The sample activity in Figure 20 integrates multiple intelligences by allowing students to select the activity that meets their area(s) of talent.

The Identification Process

> "The voice of the intellect is a soft one, but it does not rest until it has gained a hearing."
>
> —Sigmund Freud

Imagine you are preparing for a marathon. Every day you get up early and stay up extra late to run. You work tirelessly to build your stamina and improve your race time. You do strength training, sprint intervals, and follow a rigid schedule, all to prepare for that final marathon. The identification stage is like the marathon in this process. All of the steps up until this point have been made to prepare potentially gifted ELLs to be ready for the identification process. As a teacher, you have developed a deep understanding of your students and their needs, built a strong culture of advocacy, collaborated with support staff, offered various methods to ignite gifts and talents, and established a strong relationship with your ELL families. This has all been your marathon training, and now the time has finally come to put all of that hard work together to hopefully identify some of your gifted ELLs. But what is the identification process?

Figure 20
Sample Activity to Integrate Multiple Intelligences Into Content Activities

Content Standard: Identify the main ideas from a text using supporting details (grades 2–7).

Teacher Preparation: Select a meaty text that represents children who look like your students. The following are some great texts for consideration:

Grade Levels	Lexile	Guided Reading Level	Title	Author
2–3	600	P	Alvin Ho series	Lenore Look
2–3	750	P	EllRay Jakes series	Sally Warner
2–4	560	O	*Jasmine Toguchi, Mochi Queen*	Debbi Michiko Florence
2–5	670	P	Anna Hibiscus series	Atinuke
2–5	530	Q	Get Ready for Gabí series	Marissa Montes
2–5	720	M	*Lola Levine Is Not Mean*	Monica Brown
2–5	720		Precious Ramotswe Mysteries series	Alexander McCall Smith
2–5	570		The No. 1 Car Spotter series	Atinuke
2–5	590	O	*The Year of the Book*	Andrea Cheng
2–7	640		*Sherlock Sam and the Missing Heirloom in Katong*	A.J. Low
3–5	580	P	*Book Uncle and Me*	Uma Krishnaswami
3–5	820	P	*Indian Shoes*	Cynthia Leitich Smith

Figure 20, *continued*

Grade Levels	Lexile	Guided Reading Level	Title	Author
3–5	550	O	Zapato Power series	Jacqueline Jules
4–5	800–899	P	*Juana and Lucas*	Juana Medina

Then, offer the following assignment choices for students to select the activity that suits them best:

▶ **Logical-mathematical:** Create a timeline of the main events using details from the text as evidence.

▶ **Visual-spatial:** Create a comic strip of the main events and include key quotes from characters that correspond with that main event.

▶ **Musical:** Write a song to explain the main idea of the text. It should include key details from the text.

▶ **Bodily-kinesthetic:** Prepare a dance, mime, or play to explain the main ideas of the text. It can include creative methods to express the key details from the text.

▶ **Interpersonal:** Within your learning team, create a 3-D model to show the main idea of the text with key details from the text.

▶ **Intrapersonal:** Write the main idea of the text, including key details.

The identification process is a multiphase process that is used to determine which students need services outside of the regular curriculum. Ultimately, the identification process determines who is eligible and who is not eligible for gifted programs based on each student's needs, as determined from collected data points. Many districts and states use both objective and subjective data points to evaluate and measure a student's gifts and talents (see Table 8).

Table 8

Objective and Subjective Data to Evaluate Students' Gifts and Talents

Objective/Quantitative Data	Subjective/Qualitative Data
▸ Academic tests ▸ Achievement tests ▸ IQ tests ▸ Student's past academic and performance record	▸ Teacher/parent rating scales ▸ Student portfolios ▸ Teacher/parent nominations ▸ Observational data of the student

Both the subjective and the objective data points are then used to evaluate a student's abilities within the multiphase process. The phases are typically (1) identification phase, (2) screening or selection phase, and (3) placement phase. Because a student may never reach Phase 3 without first passing Phase 1 and Phase 2, all key players must work together to give the potentially gifted ELL as many opportunities as possible to pass the earlier phases (NAGC & Council of State Directors of Programs for the Gifted, 2015).

Ideally, the identification process would involve a team of the key players, such as the classroom teacher, ELL teacher, AIG teacher, and parent, coming together to determine if a student needs additional support because of their above-average behaviors. In this same ideal world, all children who are performing above grade-level expectations would be eligible for gifted programs. However, this is not the case for many reasons.

Why Aren't More ELLs Identified as Gifted?

Many of the problems that gifted ELLs face directly tie back to the identification process. What aspects of the identification process make it challenging for CLED students?

▸ **Confusion about the purpose of identification:** Some view identification as a reward for good behavior, similar to the shy or quiet overachiever. Others view it as a means to recognize and idolize students with Americanized values, thus overlooking CLED students. Students who are great leaders making positive, visible impacts toward those around them may be identified as gifted because their values align with widely held views of gifts and talents within American culture. However, this discounts how giftedness appears in other cultures and therefore reaffirms existing perceptions of giftedness.

▸ **Lack of educational equity:** Underrepresented populations struggle to be identified by programs that are solely dependent on academic achievement assessments. According to the National Report on Identification (Alvino et al., 1981), academic achievement assessments led to the exclusion of students with learning disabilities, creative and divergent thinking, culturally or linguistically diverse backgrounds, and low socioeconomic status (SES).

▸ **Elitist views of giftedness:** Many schools use elitist definitions of giftedness that lead to predominantly White, middle class students being recognized as gifted while also disregarding other groups (Castellano, 2002).

▸ **Selective referrals:** More often than not, CLED students are not considered for gifted programs because of widely held beliefs and deficit thinking regarding CLED students. This thinking might include comments such as, "They can't be gifted or receive enrichment; they don't know English yet." The factors that contribute to this deficit line of thinking include low academic expectations by teachers, lack of teacher training, limited cultural considerations, and inability to recognize talents in CLED students (Castellano, 2002).

▸ **Socioeconomic disadvantages:** Students attending schools in low-income areas face increased rates for violent crime, fewer educational opportunities, and higher risks of dropping out (Parrett & Budge, 2016). They also are more likely to be taught by inexperienced teachers or teachers facing burnout (Long, 2015). Many of these schools struggle to control behavioral concerns to teach remedial concepts, leaving limited time, energy, and resources to support gifted CLED students. Because these schools are constantly "putting out everyday fires," staff has limited time and ability to support the needs of gifted CLED students.

▶ **Improper implementation of identification instruments:** Tests, such as IQ tests and achievement tests, are being improperly used to identify or exclude students for gifted programs. These include the SAT and the Woodcock Johnson Reading Mastery Tests. The purpose of these assessment instruments is to determine placement in a course or within a program. Many states and local educational agencies use student performance on standardized assessments, such as intelligence or achievement tests, as their singular measurement tool for the identification of gifted learners (Runge & McGowan, 2012). However, the use of these instruments for identification leads to the exclusion of CLED students (Alvino et al., 1981). Reliance on IQ scores alone is a major cause of demographic homogeneity in gifted and talented programs (Harris et al., 2009).

▶ **After-the-fact data collection:** This takes place when parents are asked for insight about their child after the student has been nominated or referred for gifted program consideration. Teachers might also be asked to consider gifts and talents of only students who have entered the talent pool (based on high achievement on standardized assessments). This results in fewer CLED students being considered because parents and teachers never thought or knew to consider them for gifted programming (Castellano, 2002).

▶ **Test bias:** Research indicates a longstanding foundation of discrimination toward CLED individuals within standardized assessments. This goes back to America's history of standardized testing dating back to World War I. Standardized tests were used to sort soldiers by their mental abilities in preparation for war (Gershon, 2015). Additional research indicates that these tests are created and geared toward White, middle, or upper-class populations (Castellano, 1998; Frasier & Passow, 1994).

▶ **Skewed data analysis:** Multiple data points are collected to consider students' gifts and talents, which is an excellent step toward identifying more gifted ELLs. However, these data points are easily skewed during the analysis of the data because the data may be unreliable, weighted in favor of or against certain groups, or incorrectly placed within a matrix using other data (Castellano, 2002).

▸ **Emphasis on Americanized definitions of giftedness:** Values of giftedness vary from culture to culture, as previously discussed, often excluding variations in giftedness from other cultures. Americanized definitions of giftedness stress the importance of high IQ and academic achievement, thereby excluding students with varied learning needs. These include students with above-average IQs who are underachieving within the regular curriculum due to disinterest or lack of challenge, as well as creative students who do not meet IQ or achievement criteria (Castellano, 2002).

▸ **Fear or focus on status quo:** Due to budget cuts across educational programs, competition for educational resources is at an all-time high, including positions and programs for the gifted. Some leaders and parents believe that if ethnic/racial minority groups enter gifted programs, it may cause more dominant groups to become excluded. According to Castellano (2002), "many administrators argue that because of limited resources, only a small number can be served" (p. 101).

▸ **Lack of teacher training to identify gifts and talents:** Research indicates that most educational programs for teachers at the university level do little to train teachers on gifted learning (Tomlinson, 2014). The average teacher may have only one course on gifted learning throughout their studies. As teachers enter the classroom to teach students, including students with gifted abilities, they are ill-prepared to recognize gifts and talents, let alone gifts and talents of CLED students. This issue is compounded by teachers' inexperience with cultural differences that affect learning styles.

Only 30 states require specific criteria to identify students for gifted programs, and those criteria vary greatly from state to state, as there is no set federal criteria for the identification of or programming for gifted learners (McGowan et al., 2016). So, what is being done to support gifted ELLs to become identified?

Successful Efforts in Increasing the Number of Identified Gifted ELLs

Over the past few decades, several research groups, organizations, and the U.S. government have sought to level the playing field for gifted ELLs to become enrolled in gifted education programs. Some of the most successful efforts include Project GOTCHA, Project CLUE, Project TOPS, and Fairfax County Public Schools in Virginia:

► **Project GOTCHA (Galaxies of Thinking and Creative Heights of Achievement):** This former Title VII academic excellence program was funded by the Office of Bilingual Education and Minority Language Affairs (OBEMLA) under the U.S. Department of Education. It was created and implemented to better meet the needs of high-ability learners who were not yet proficient in English. The project's program took place between 1987 and 1996 across 15 states and used a multifaceted approach for the identification of potentially gifted ELLs using a set of special criteria. Among the criteria included were teacher nomination, analysis of creative ability, students' thinking skills, and student leadership. The specific criteria are notable because they must be observed or noted by the classroom teacher, meaning that the ELL must demonstrate characteristics of giftedness within their classroom setting. The results of these criteria were recorded for a gifted ELL committee to discuss and determine students' eligibility. This resulted in 41% of the students being eligible based on criteria set by the state (Aguirre, 2003).

► **Project CLUE:** This project, which took place in Indianapolis schools, used the following identification criteria so that any student could enter the identification pool process if they met either of the following conditions:

  ► Part 1—Students who scored in the 90th percentile or above on the TerraNova test.

  ► Part 2—Students who score in the 90th percentile on any of the TerraNova subtests.

Any students who didn't meet either of those criteria moved on to Part 3:

▷ Part 3—Students were administered the Raven's Colored Progressive Matrices (Raven CPM-C), a group administered, nonverbal test of fluid intelligence. Students scoring at or above the 90th percentile on the Raven CPM-C also then entered the identification pool. Additionally, all students were evaluated using the fourth and final criterion.

▷ Part 4—Parents and/or teachers completed an experimenter-designed teacher or parent rating scale called the Adams-Pierce Checklist (APC), available in English and Spanish, to identify any students who may have been missed by the first three criteria.

This identification process is known as a "sift down" process because it uses a multiple-measures approach for identification that continues across multiple levels to catch any and all potentially gifted learners. Project CLUE resulted in an increase of identified gifted ELLs by 9% (Pierce et al., 2006).

▶ **Project TOPS (Teacher Observation of Potential in Students):** This study took place across four states and included more than 100 Title I schools. The purpose of the program was to shift teacher thinking from a deficit mindset to a dynamic mindset of culturally and linguistically diverse student populations. It used the materials from the Using Science, Talents, and Abilities to Recognize Students—Promoting Learning for Underrepresented Students (U-STARS~PLUS) program. Over the first 3–6 weeks, teachers observed the students using a protocol after receiving training from a whole-class perspective. During the next 3–6 weeks, teachers used the Independent Student Observation form to look for potentially gifted students. The study resulted in 436 CLED students being identified who would have been excluded without this program, according to teacher interviews. The 436 CLED students included African American boys and Latinos of both genders (Cross & Dockery, 2014).

▸ **Fairfax County Public Schools in Virginia:** This school district successfully created and implemented a program to identify underrepresented gifted students, including those from low-income backgrounds, English language learners, and twice-exceptional learners. The program consisted of a multi-faceted approach that included differentiated classroom services, direct instruction from the AIG teacher, and full-time programming with daily challenging instruction. This resulted in a 565% increase in the number of Black and Latino students receiving high school gifted services 11 years after implementation (Virginia Department of Education, 2017).

These examples confirm that it is possible to increase the number of identified gifted ELLs in large, urban areas as well as smaller, rural areas across the country. In a review of the literature by NCRGE (Mun et al., 2016), researchers found that using a multiple-measures identification process was the most effective method for increasing the identification of gifted ELLs. They suggested the following methods to be the most effective:

▸ modifying the identification procedures;
▸ preparing students for advanced content and critical thinking;
▸ implementing curriculum/instructional changes with an emphasis on addressing culturally, linguistically, and/or economically diverse student needs;
▸ cultivating relationships between ELL families and school personnel, such as classroom teachers and support staff; and
▸ developing plans for gifted program evaluation.

Many of these success stories include the factor of assessments. The following assessments have been proven to be effective for identifying gifted ELLs:

▸ **Raven's Progressive Matrices (RPM):** This is a nonverbal, standardized, group-administered assessment for identifying gifts and talents through abstract reasoning and nonverbal intelligence. According to Saccuzzo & Johnson (1995), replacing the Wechsler assessment with the RPM within a large, urban school district resulted in an increase of 7 times the number of identified Latinos in the gifted program over a 3-year period.

▶ **Standard Progressive Matrices (SPM):** This standardized nonverbal instrument is one of the three assessments within the RPM. It can be administered in a group or individual setting to assess abstract reasoning and nonverbal intelligence. The school district of Palm Beach County, FL, found success in its implementation across 10 Title I elementary schools. The use of the SPM resulted in an increase in the number of eligible CLED students in each of those 10 schools within one year (Castellano, 2002).

▶ **Naglieri Nonverbal Ability Test (NNAT):** This is also a standardized nonverbal instrument that assesses reasoning and general problem-solving skills. It has been shown to be effective for increasing the number of eligible CLED students for gifted programs in multiple districts (Castellano, 2002).

▶ **Cognitive Abilities Test (CogAT):** This is a group-administered K–12 assessment intended to estimate students' learned reasoning and problem-solving abilities through a battery of verbal, quantitative, and nonverbal assessments. Charlotte-Mecklenburg Schools in North Carolina have seen a substantial increase in the number of identified underrepresented students within the gifted program with the usage of this instrument in conjunction with other data criteria (Public Schools of North Carolina, n.d.).

▶ **Hispanic Bilingual Gifted Screening Instrument (HBGSI):** This is a 78-item checklist for teachers to use to evaluate Latino students' talents on a 5-point scale. It has been shown to be effective in Southwest schools in the U.S. (Castellano, 2002).

If your district or state elects to create or purchase a new assessment, key factors to consider to ensure that the assessment is equitable for CLED students include (1) content validity, (2) construct validity, and (3) predictive validity. This is represented in Figure 21. Content validity can ensure that selected assessments are unbiased toward any group. Good suggestions for this area include nonverbal assessments, as they

Figure 21
Assessment Instrument Considerations

Content validity	Construct validity	Predictive validity
► Does the assessment measure the intended content area?	► Does the instrument measure the intended construct, trait, or behavior? What constructs are used to define intelligence?	► Is the instrument used to predict individuals' future success or failure?

reduce the background knowledge and academic vocabulary necessary to demonstrate abilities. Content validity ensures that the assessment measures the target area without bias. An example of bias could be: *Intelligence means having strong expressive skills, so a child who can clearly express themselves better than others is considered intelligent.* This example is obviously skewed toward expressive skills, and thereby excludes those without strong expressive skills. This example reaffirms the importance of the construct of the assessment. Nonverbal assessments have been shown to identify CLED students for gifted programs because they reduce the disparities in IQ tests between monolingual and bilingual students, reduce oral and written language requirements, and fairly measure abilities for students of all backgrounds.

For Teachers, Administrators, and District/State Leaders

Provide *Equitable, Not Equal* Opportunities for the Identification of Gifted ELLs. Research indicates that using a multiple-method approach for identification of gifted learners provides equitable opportunities for CLED and underrepresented students to be eligible for gifted programs (Castellano, 2002; Ford, 2011; Kitano & Pedersen, 2002, Mun et al., 2016; NAGC, 2010). But what is a multiple-methods or multicriteria approach? Both of these approaches require the use of multiple criteria to evaluate a students' talents and abilities, rather than

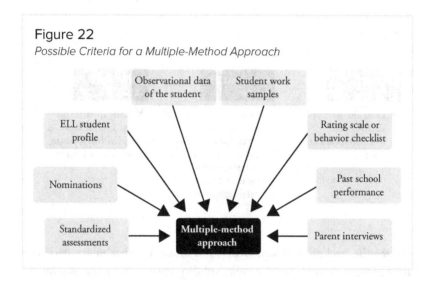

Figure 22
Possible Criteria for a Multiple-Method Approach

relying on one academic or achievement assessment. They also usually include a "sift down" or funnel process in which a student has multiple opportunities to demonstrate gifts and talents that are then evaluated as a whole picture of that child. This suggests that a funnel approach of identifying students can help educators consider a wider range of students for gifted programs.

Figure 22 presents an array of methods and criteria that can be used to increase the number of CLED and underrepresented students in gifted programs. Standardized assessments may include aptitude and achievement, especially if they are administered in the students' native language, as appropriate. Teachers, parents, peers, and community or cultural groups that are relevant to the students can make student nominations. Student work samples can include a portfolio and writing samples.

Despite the opportunities that a multiple-method or multiple-criteria approach affords, the data points are meaningless if they are not evaluated using certain student considerations. The evaluation of the data must take place through a team of evaluators using established rubrics. Evaluation teams may consist of one or more AIG teachers and an ELL teacher, and may include district-level support. The key to the team's analysis of the data is to look at CLED students individually, rather than comparing them to native speakers. It is also essential for the evaluative team to look at each student as a whole, considering cultural background, growth in language proficiency, and the student's current language proficiency. Therefore, it is recommended that the ELL teacher support the collection of data points for ELLs, as well as create a profile for ELLs to be considered during the evaluation team's final analysis of the multiple data points.

An ELL student profile should consist of (1) a brief introduction of the student, (2) the student's current language proficiency, and (3) a comparison in their language growth from one year to the next. The student introduction should include whether or not the student was born the in the U.S., how many years they have been in U.S. schools, their family background, and the student's cultural background. The introduction of the ELL helps to paint a picture of their motivation, leadership skills, emotional needs, and methods of expression. Next, the student's current language proficiency is meant to serve as an index of how that student should be performing, based on their current language levels. For example, if a student is a novice ELL, based on their current language proficiency, but they are able to write multiple sentences or explain their problem-solving skills for a math question using specific vocabulary, this shows that the student is performing above their current language proficiency. The final data point for the profile, a comparison of the student's language growth from one year to the next, shows whether the student is able to develop language proficiency at a faster pace than their peers. Accelerated language development can be an excellent indicator of an ELL's gifts and talents. However, a student's lack of accelerated language development is not an indicator that they are not gifted. Multiple factors may affect a student's language development; therefore, the combination of the three data points can help paint a holistic understanding of the ELL's learning profile to support the evaluation team in its assessment of the ELL's gifts, talents, and academic needs.

Additional research has found the following criteria to be effective in identifying CLED and underrepresented students for gifted programs:

- ▸ Consider alternative evaluative criteria for ELLs (Hamayan & Damico, 1991), such as portfolios, parent nominations, and teacher data.

- ▸ Consider students' cultural background and linguistic progress, such as motivation, speed of language acquisition, and vocabulary usage in writing based on their current language proficiency.
- ▸ Provide an array of activities for CLED students to accurately represent their talents (Armour-Thomas, 1992).
- ▸ Use equitable assessments that do not penalize students based on gender, culture, or other bias (LaCelle-Peterson & Rivera, 1994).
- ▸ Ensure equitable access to assessments for CLED students by providing testing accommodations, such as testing in the students' native language when appropriate, extended time for testing, and breaks as needed.
- ▸ Provide ongoing teacher training on gifted behaviors and how to nurture them, as well as the role of cultural backgrounds within gifted constructs.
- ▸ Consider multiple areas of giftedness, such as intellectual giftedness, academic giftedness, academic intellectual giftedness, academic math giftedness, and academic reading giftedness.

Ultimately, the goal of a multiple-method or multiple-criteria approach is to ensure equity for all students to be identified for gifted programs. There are several advantages for using a multiple-measure approach for identification, such as increased accountability, equitable access to programs, and opportunities for program development (Castellano, 2002). Therefore, state and district leaders should consider the usage of multiple data points for student evaluation, as well as the means for evaluating those data points, to ensure validity and impartiality.

Using an RtI/MTSS Approach for Identification. Using Response to Intervention (RtI) or Multi-Tiered Systems of Support (MTSS) for gifted program identification can offer additional opportunities for CLED students. Curriculum-based measures are used in current models to identify students with potential learning disabilities and at-risk students, and researchers have proposed using a similar approach of RtI for gifted students (Bianco & Harris, 2014; McGowan et al., 2016). According to NAGC (2010), the same methods used by RtI teams could be used to identify and serve gifted children, as RtI aligns with the best practices for the identification, assessment, and programming for gifted learners.

RtI and MTSS are three-tiered processes to identify students needing additional academic support. Tier 1 instruction is the general classroom instruction from the general education teacher for all students. Tier 2 instruction is provided to students who are not making adequate growth within the general classroom at Tier 1. Tier 2 instruction gives students with academic needs additional instruction in the needed area for a set amount of time each week, using research-based interventions. After a set amount of time, if a student is still not meeting their growth expectation, the student may be moved to a Tier 3 level of support. Tier 3 instruction provides the student with a more intense direct instruction plan in the academic area of need. For example, a student at Tier 2 may receive direct instruction in a small group 3 days a week. The same student, when moved to Tier 3, may transition to a one-on-one setting for the same 3 days a week. Another example may be a Tier 2 student who received direct instruction in a small group setting for 15 minutes for 3 days a week; the student may then move to Tier 3, receiving direct instruction in the same small group for 5 days a week for 15 minutes, or for 3 days a week for 30 minutes, if the others in the small group were also moved to Tier 3. The purpose of Tier 3 interventions is to increase the amount of direct instruction in the academic area of need to help that child meet their growth expectation. Transitioning from Tier 2 to Tier 3 may include moving to a one-on-one setting or increasing the time or frequency of direct instruction. The goal of the entire tier plan process is to help the student to achieve their academic growth and proficiency goals. However, it can also be used to identify students with additional learning needs, which may lead to screening for possible learning disabilities.

This same model for support and possible identification can be used as a strength-based approach to identify potentially gifted ELLs. Research indicates that using a strength-based RtI or MTSS process can increase the number of identified gifted ELLs for enrollment in gifted programs (Bianco & Harris, 2014). In a strength-based model, Tier 1 still refers to the general classroom instruction and lessons with the addition of support from a gifted education specialist. Tier 2 interventions are used for students who demonstrate a need for enrichment learning because they may demonstrate mastery or an accelerated pace for learning. After a set amount of time, Tier 3 interventions can be implemented for high-achieving students who demonstrate a need for additional academic enrichment beyond Tier 2. Interventions at this level may include accelerated learning programs, testing out methods for students who demonstrate mastery, learning contracts, or student-created learning pathways.

Similar to the traditional RtI or MTSS model, interventions can be created in collaboration with the ELL teacher, AIG teacher, classroom teacher, student, and parent. The purpose of the strength-based interventions is to allow the student to explore the core curriculum at an accelerated pace or in greater depth after considering their interests, their abilities, and the curriculum.

For a gifted ELL, this may look like mastery in math with a demonstrated need for support in reading comprehension. The RtI or MTSS team may create an educational plan through which this student receives strength-based interventions in math and targeted interventions in decoding or vocabulary. Ultimately, the purpose of any educational plan is to meet the student where they are by offering foundational support or extension support when needed. The strength-based model for RtI can support professional learning communities to consider the needs of students through structured and strategic educational plans.

Chapter Summary

Action steps continue to build upon the work of the previous chapters to nurture observed gifts and talents through a culture of advocacy. This chapter focused on the importance of the gradual release process to guide students to become independent thinkers. As students learn to become independent thinkers, they can facilitate their own learning. Educators must also implement differentiated lessons and activities, as well as design activities that allow students to demonstrate multiple intelligences through varied methods to show mastery. The purpose of nurturing gifts and talents is to allow students opportunities to develop and finesse their skills to challenge themselves within the curriculum with critical and deep thinking. The end goal of nurturing gifts and talents is to support students with their individual learning needs. For potentially gifted ELLs and underrepresented students, this means helping them to become identified and eligible for gifted programs.

This chapter also explored the process of identification of gifted ELLs for gifted programs. Because gifted programs are not federally defined or mandated, the identification process is often left to each state or district's discretion. The research presented here is meant to serve as a starting point for districts with a wide gap between identified gifted learners and identified gifted English language learners. The research intends to bolster and offer suggestions for additional improvements for districts or states that are already implementing revised gifted program plans that cast a wider net for underrepresented student populations. Lastly, the research can be used by administrators, classroom teachers, ELL teachers, and AIG teachers to support the identification of CLED students.

Discussion Questions

1. What action steps have you taken prior to this chapter to support, plan, and listen for potentially gifted ELLs?
2. Based on observational data of your gifted ELLs, what are your next steps to nurture their gifts and talents?
3. What is your school, district, or state's gifted program plan for identification?
4. What can you do to improve your gifted program plan to identify gifted ELLs?
5. What are your next steps to prepare your gifted ELLs for identification?

CHAPTER 5

Teach

How to Teach Identified Gifted ELLs

> "I have come to believe that a great teacher is a great artist and that there are as few as there are any other great artists. Teaching might even be the greatest of the arts since the medium is the human mind and spirit."
>
> —John Steinbeck

Now that you have identified gifted ELLs, how do you effectively teach them to ensure that they are academically challenged and actively engaged in their learning? Many identified gifted ELLs will drop out of gifted programs, or school altogether, if certain criteria are not met (Stambaugh & Chandler, 2012). Even though there have been positive trends to identify more ELLs as gifted and an increase in the entry of ELLs into gifted programs, there is a strong need to support them after identification. According to Stambaugh and Chandler (2012), the greatest factors that cause gifted ELLs to drop out of the program are:

- peer ridicule,
- proximity to cultural peer groups, and
- absence or minimal usage of students' interests and strengths within the curriculum content.

Research indicates that gifted ELLs are more likely to drop out of gifted programs if they are not afforded culturally responsive learning opportunities, including interactive learning with other CLED peers, engagement in the community, and participation in extracurriculars outside of the school day (Stambaugh & Chandler, 2012). It is crucial for key players to be knowledgeable and equipped to teach gifted ELLs to best meet their individual needs. These key players include parents; the ELL, AIG, and classroom teachers; and administrators and district/ state leaders. This chapter explores how to teach identified gifted ELLs through research-based practices and how parents can best support their gifted learners at home. It also explores the strategy of bibliotherapy and a growth mindset to support gifted children's socioemotional needs.

Supporting Identified Gifted ELLs Using Research-Based Practices and Curriculum

"My mission in life is not merely to survive, but to thrive; and to do so with some passion, some compassion, some humor, and some style."

—Maya Angelou

Research suggests an increasing need to support the socioemotional needs of children, often referred to as the whole child, to best meet their learning needs (Genesee, 2011; Rasberry et al., 2015). The purpose of supporting the whole child is to learn about not only their learning interests or styles, but also what makes that child feel complete, including their family or home life, their personal journeys, or family relationships. It is easy to get lost in the data of students' learning while forgetting simple human essentials. Parents want their children to have opportunities for the best future possible. Teachers want their students to have opportunities to grow and thrive. Administrators want their students to have equal opportunities to be successful, and district/state leaders want to facilitate the process to make it possible for any learner to become college- or career-ready. This section explores each key player's role in this process and how to carry out that role.

For Parents

Now that your child has been identified as eligible for a gifted program, there are a number of ways to best support their needs. Those considerations include outside-of-school supports, schooling options, program options, and socioemotional needs.

Outside-of-School Enrichment Options. These options may include extracurricular activities, mentorships, career exploration, travel, and do-nothing time.

- ▸ **Extracurricular activities:** Examples across different areas of interest might include:
    - ▹ music—learning a new instrument, joining a choir, or developing music using electronic tools such as Garage Band;
    - ▹ physical activity—sports, dance, gymnastics, martial arts, golf, etc.;
    - ▹ theater—playwriting, developing sounds for a production, actors' makeup, stage effects;
    - ▹ art—painting, drawing, sculpture, pottery, photography;
    - ▹ crafts—woodworking, sewing, interior design, model building;
    - ▹ recreational reading;
    - ▹ writing—stories, poems, biographies, research articles;
    - ▹ language learning experiences—study abroad, language immersion, language coffee hours;
    - ▹ performance theater—attending concerts or showcases in different artistic media;
    - ▹ math and science—engineering programs or camps;
    - ▹ computer learning—coding, website development, and design;
    - ▹ community service—health-related associations, global causes, political affiliations, marches, etc.;

> leadership opportunities—tutoring, interest groups, religious or community organizations;
> clubs—chess, cooking, photography, robotics;
> camps—summer or recreational camps (e.g., sailing, baking, horseback riding); and
> competitions—local, regional, national, international levels in different subject areas (D. J. Matthews & Foster, 2005, pp. 158–159).

- **Mentorships:** A mentor is someone who could offer support in an interest to younger students or peers. A mentee is someone receiving the support. A gifted student could benefit from both having a mentor in their area of interest as well as serving as a mentor for younger students needing support. The benefits of being a mentor or mentee include:
  > real-world application of knowledge or skills,
  > developing new connections,
  > increased learning within the field of interest from a different perspective,
  > relationship-building experience,
  > shared respect for both the mentor (for showcasing expertise) and mentee (for being valued),
  > an increase in career path awareness, and
  > feelings of involvement and enjoyment.

  Concerns to consider when developing a mentorship include:
  > proper learning environment for both the mentor and mentee to feel welcome and safe;
  > the student's learning interest (Is the area for mentorship something that both the mentee and mentor feel is important?);
  > expertise in the field (Does the gifted student work well with others who may have more knowledge in the field? Does the student have the patience to work with someone who may not have as much expertise in an area?);

> time commitment (Does the gifted student have the time needed for this learning experience, either to teach someone else or to gain new experiences/knowledge for themselves?);

> learning style (Does the gifted student work well with others who may learn or teach differently than how they learn or teach best?);

> personality, including emotional and social temperament and ability to work with others; and

> motivation (Does the student have the necessary self-management, commitment, and responsibility skills for this task?; D. J. Matthews & Foster, 2005, pp. 162–163).

▶ **Career exploration:** Opportunities might include:

> internships;

> volunteering at an occupational site, such as a camp for interest in teaching, computer store for technology interests, or a law office for legal interests;

> job shadowing; or

> watching TED Talks in a field of interest.

▶ **Travel:** Travel promotes awareness of other customs, cultures, and/or beliefs. Travel can be supported with students' use or application of:

> travel magazines or travel books on the area being explored;

> studying maps or atlases;

> exploring new areas through hiking, bike riding, kayaking, skiing, or other means that are unique to certain areas;

> guiding discussion on similarities and differences between new areas and home, including food, clothing, architecture, or history;

> a diary or travel journal to record thoughts or feelings as they see and learn new information about an area; and

> discussing various questions over the course of a trip to a new area to spark higher order thinking, such as "What is your favorite thing about this town or area? What aspects of life here do you like better than life at home, and why?"

(e.g., eating dinner at 10 p.m. in southern Spain versus 7 p.m. at home).

▸ **Do-nothing time:** Allow for there to be time when your child has nothing to do. This means they cannot be on electronic devices or be given a book or activity. This time allows your child to reflect and ignite their imagination and creativity. Without boredom, many inventions would never have been created. It is okay if your child complains that they are bored. This is good because it means that they will have to activate their own imagination or creativity (D. J. Matthews & Foster, 2005, p. 170).

Schooling Options. As a parent, especially for a gifted learner needing additional support in the right areas to maximize their learning potential, you want to ensure that your child has the best education possible. The following are a few considerations when choosing a gifted program (D. J. Matthews & Foster, 2005).

▸ **Teacher considerations:**
  ▹ Are you able to observe a lesson or be a classroom helper? If you are not allowed to observe a classroom, figure out why. If the reasoning is to reduce the amount of classroom distractions or disruptions, this is understandable. In this case, you may offer to be a classroom helper to get a better feel of the school's learning environment. If nothing else, the school should be able to give you a tour of the facility or building to give you a better picture of the learning environment.
  ▹ Do teachers hold advanced degrees or have their National Board Certification?
  ▹ Do teachers listen to the needs and/or concerns of children, parents, and other teachers? It is crucial that teachers are receptive to a child's learning needs, with some exceptions. Teachers do not need to respond to every possible concern, such as tattling, concerns about line order, or which student turned in a paper first. However, a teacher

must respond when a child is hurt, bullied, or ignored. As a parent, you want to establish an open forum for communication for the teacher's concerns/needs as well as your own.

- Do teachers promote humor and a sense of curiosity?
- Are teachers concerned with more than test scores to get to know the whole child?

- **Program/curricular considerations:**
  - Are there clear, rigorous, and accessible academic content standards posted in the classroom?
  - Are there opportunities for peer collaboration?
  - Do students have opportunities for creative expression?
  - Is there a visible acceptance of diverse cultures and learning?
  - Are there opportunities for critical thinking and time for students to grapple with content?
  - Do teachers establish mutual respect between themselves and students?
  - Are students actively engaged with their learning, or are they passive?
  - Is differentiation and scaffolding evident in lessons?

- **Administrative considerations:**
  - Are administrators open and receptive toward your concerns?
  - Are administrators supportive, sensitive, and nurturing toward potentially gifted learners?
  - How do administrators support teacher knowledge and collaboration for the best instructional practices of gifted learners?

Socioemotional Needs. The following are some general guidelines for parents of gifted children:

- Be patient and tolerant of potentially impolite or long lines of questioning (e.g., the incessant "but why?" comments).
- Be open and receptive to your child's interests.
- Encourage your child's curiosity and imagination.
- Play with your child.

- ▶ Provide learning choices for them to decide what they want to learn next.
- ▶ Offer guidance and insight for healthy peer relationships.
- ▶ Let your child fail to a reasonable extent to let them explore their own limitations.
- ▶ Guide your child to set attainable goals.
- ▶ Provide and promote age-appropriate learning opportunities, such as the enrichment activities listed previously (D. J. Matthews & Foster, 2005, p. 267).

For Teachers: Best Practices and Teaching Strategies

As a teacher with many tasks on your already-packed plate, how do you add one more? The easiest answer is to recognize that it is not adding another piece to your plate, but instead adding a tool to your toolkit. This section helps you answer the question of how to challenge and meet the needs of your students by providing the methods to do so. Many of these strategies, although aimed at supporting gifted ELLs, are best practices for all learners. Research has found a number of strategies to be particularly useful in gifted ELL instruction, including:

- ▶ incorporate student strengths;
- ▶ maintain high expectations for students through challenging content;
- ▶ incorporate opportunities for critical thinking skills, such as deductive reasoning, and argumentative, evaluative, or analogical thinking skills (VanTassel-Baska & Stambaugh, 2016);
- ▶ encourage independent thinking and open inquiry;
- ▶ facilitate student problem solving and student-directed work;
- ▶ use bilingual cooperative learning teams (Robisheaux & Banbury, 2002);
- ▶ set up mentor pairs to support struggling students;
- ▶ employ student-centered approaches that promote active learning;
- ▶ emphasize oral and written language development; and
- ▶ value students' languages, cultures, and experiences (Kitano & Pedersen, 2002).

In addition to these best practices, four strategies stand out as being the most impactful for gifted ELLs. The "Fantastic Four Teaching Strategies" are routines, bibliotherapy, team building, and a growth mindset. These strategies can instantly transform your classroom dynamic and ensure that your gifted ELLs feel safe, welcome, and happy to be there.

Establish Routines. One of my favorite best practices is establishing routines for students to become acclimated to teacher expectations. Routines establish a sense of calm and reduce student anxieties. This is particularly helpful for CLED students who may face daily life challenges, such as limited food and shelter, or who have experienced these hardships in the past. By setting up a framework for the flow of the class structure through routines, students feel welcome, secure, and safe in their learning environment. Some of the routines that I have used in the past include startup and closing routines. My startup routine is what I expect students to do upon entry into the classroom; these mostly stay the same for the duration of the year. Some of these expectations include student choice for flexible seating, problem solving to find and locate materials, and forming student learning teams. By having choices in their learning, students become independent, free, and critical thinkers—crucial aspects of being 21st-century learners. Similar to the gradual release process, you should only teach a few expectations per day while constantly reinforcing previously taught expectations until students have content mastered. Afterward, actively observe your students' work processes to ensure that they are meeting your expectations.

Use Bibliotherapy. Bibliotherapy is a tool to help readers cope with personal problems through characters in a text that are similar to them. This concept will be explored in greater detail later in the chapter. This fantastic tool can (Adderholdt-Elliott & Eller, 1989):

- guide student reflection and provide insight into past or future situations,
- broaden student's social and emotional competency for handling certain situations,
- strengthen home and school connections,
- prevent loneliness or feelings of rejection,

▶ address feelings of frustration or impatience with others who may not be gifted,

▶ illustrate different methods for handling challenging peer interactions,

▶ explore and teach coping strategies for children with anxieties regarding perfectionism and idealism,

▶ support peaceful relaxation, and

▶ provide a structured and safe outlet for those who feel different.

Integrate Team-Building Opportunities. Humans are creatures of habit and comfort, and this is true in the classroom setting. Students want to be welcome, accepted, and celebrated in a shared space. Data indicate that gifted ELLs are more susceptible to leave gifted programs than other populations because of isolationism factors (Stambaugh & Chandler, 2012). Gifted ELLs encounter this isolationism because they originally have their schooling with like-peers, or friends from their community. However, once they are in gifted programs, they are likely to be separated from their peers and become an extreme minority within the gifted program. It is important for gifted ELLs to feel welcome, accepted, and celebrated. One team-building task card activity that can support new gifted ELLs is Let's Get Together, Yeah, Yeah, Yeah (With a Hint of Figurative Language)" available at https://www.prufrock.com/Identifying-and-Supporting-Gifted-English-Language-Learners-Resources.aspx. This activity requires students to work in pairs to read various task cards and then fill in the missing blank to form a complete sentence. Some of the sentences on the task cards are quotes from famous movies, while others are fill-in-the-blanks using figurative language. This activity allows students to feel welcome while being academically challenged.

Fostering a Growth Mindset. A growth mindset refers to a learner's ability to always seek areas for growth rather than shying away from failure or mistakes, referred to as fixed mindset. Fostering a growth mindset will also be explored in greater detail later in this chapter.

The Fantastic Four are all research-based teaching strategies that have been proven to be effective to support gifted ELLs. They can be easily implemented and maintained in any size classroom to ensure that gifted ELLs may flourish within a gifted program.

For Teachers, Administrators, and District/State Leaders: Gifted Program Curriculum Options

Curricular programs and models provide the framework of what to teach and, in some cases, how to teach it. Curriculum can also determine when to teach different concepts, with the end goal of being able to support students to meet or exceed content standards in proficiency and growth of knowledge. Gifted students, like all students, need to be challenged within the content, as well as with researched teaching methods and strategies (Ford, 2011). However, there are so many curricular options flooding the educational market that it is hard to know which models have been researched for proven effectiveness. The curriculum chosen impacts children on a large scale and can potentially cost millions in funding. Therefore, it is crucial that districts and states consider adopting or integrating curriculum that incorporates a wider range of support to best meet the needs of students, especially culturally diverse students. The curriculum options listed in Table 9 have been researched and proven to be effective in supporting CLED students with gifts and talents:

- ▶ **Schoolwide Enrichment Model Reading Framework (SEM-R)** is an instructional literacy strategy proven to be effective with gifted learners. It is designed for students in grades 3–5 to scaffold reading instruction. The format of the strategy is very similar to reader's workshop outlines in that it includes interest-based reading selections, teacher-guided discussion, and student goal setting and regulation during independent reading. It also incorporates differentiation of reading levels, teacher conferring, and student self-regulation to develop stronger reading behaviors (Ford, 2011).
- ▶ **Philosophy for Children** is an inquiry-based program to guide children to develop articulation skills in various disciplines and promote awareness of differing opinions. It achieves this by exploring common content, texts, and resources with students

Table 9

Curricular Program Options for Gifted ELLs

Targeted Grade/ Age Range	Curricular Program
K–5	Junior Great Books
K–8	Jacob's Ladder Reading Comprehension Program
K–12 (best for grades 6–12)	Future Problem Solving Program International
K–12	Higher Order Thinking Skills (HOTS)
K–12	Odyssey of the Mind
K–12	Philosophy for Children
K–12 (best for ages 8–13)	Schoolwide Enrichment Model Reading Framework (SEM-R)
3–6	Mentoring Mathematical Minds (M³)

and then presenting challenging thinking assignments. The program focuses on reasoning skills, inquiry skills, and critical dispositions.

▶ **Higher Order Thinking Skills (HOTS)** are skills that seek to improve a student's understanding of a concept. The target skills of HOTS include (1) creating solutions for problems and testing them out, (2) analyzing the quality of problem-solving strategies, (3) seeking outside help when needed to solve a problem, and (4) synthesizing new information to solve a problem. HOTS is also a curriculum that is available for schools and districts (see https:// higherorderthinkingschools.org/about/overview). The purpose of this curriculum is to train teachers to guide and coach students to learn problem-solving skills (Ford, 2011).

▶ **Junior Great Books** is a program that promotes literacy development using folktales to spark students' critical thinking skills, such as inferencing, drawing conclusions, and evaluating character perspectives. The texts within this program are multicultural representatives of various cultural histories and also include international authors.

- ▸ **Odyssey of the Mind** is an international team-based problem-solving program for students of all ages. It challenges students to explore and develop life skills through a series of activities that culminate with an annual competition. Some problems have included designing a mechanical dinosaur, building a working vehicle, writing a new chapter to *Moby Dick*, and turning Pandora's Box into a video game.
- ▸ **Mentoring Mathematical Minds (M³)** is an elementary math enrichment curriculum geared toward third- through sixth-grade content standards. The program integrates Common Core State Standards with higher order thinking with an easy-to-understand pacing guide, learning rubrics, and differentiated content to challenge deeper thinking within the content. According to NCRGE (Mun et al., 2016), ELLs who received the M³ intervention were found to have significantly greater gains in math achievement when compared to a group who had not.
- ▸ **Jacob's Ladder Reading Comprehension Program** is a supplemental language arts resource developed by William & Mary. It targets reading comprehension skills for high-ability learners. Some of the activities focus on sequencing, cause/effect, consequences, and implications. The activities are tiered within a passage to increase complexity and intellectual demand. Students will need structured support to build their understanding and thinking of the text with the support of the teacher (Stambaugh & VanTassel-Baska, 2018; VanTassel-Baska & Stambaugh, 2016).

Curriculum, or the content being taught, can also be modified based on students' needs. Modification options within the curriculum include:

- ▸ **Depth:** Offer greater detail and deeper understanding opportunities.
- ▸ **Breadth:** Extend a topic because of student interest.
- ▸ **Tempo:** Adjust the speed of learning as needed.
- ▸ **Expansion of basic skills and comprehension:** For students to become producers of information, they need to learn from professionals in the field of production. For example, for stu-

dents interested in science, bring in a scientist to lead an experiment; for those interested in writing, bring in an author to share about their writing process.

- ▶ **Process modifications:** Use critical and creative thinking and Bloom's (1956) taxonomy.
- ▶ **Independent study or self-selected content:** Students select topics of interest to show mastery independently.
- ▶ **Telescoping or compacting:** Give students pre- and posttests. If they already show mastery, allow them to make choices, including the option to cover a related topic.
- ▶ **Add:** Bring in extra topics that allow in-depth research in areas of interest.

Instructional approaches can be modified, such as how you deliver the content, the assignments themselves, practice time with the content, etc. The following are ways that instruction can be modified:

- ▶ **Tier assignments:** Break down assignments to incorporate higher order thinking and problem-solving skills throughout the scaffolding process rather than just as the last step.
- ▶ **Group by need:** Flexibly move students to small groups based on their need within that content area and cluster gifted students together for different activities (Hoover et al., 1993).
- ▶ **Create learning centers:** These should be self-paced, content based, and incorporate multiple intelligences such as using previously learned skills to build something or applying previous knowledge.
- ▶ **Integrate interest centers:** Expose students to areas not covered in the curriculum, such as dinosaurs, the arts, engineering, space, architecture, etc., by having a center that integrates content skills such as summarizing or explaining.
- ▶ **Create learning contracts:** Work with students to develop a learning contract that explains what they will do and when. The learning contract should be carried out independently, be self-paced, blend skill and content, and foster research and critical thinking. You will also need to cocreate a rubric with a clear expectation of mastery

▶ **Offer independent study or self-selected topic:** To implement independent study with your students, help them decide
how they will demonstrate mastery and their expectations for
learning their self-selected topic. A good practice is to make
sure to include a presentation component.

Additional program choices for your gifted program can include:
▶ **Resource room/enrichment center:** Create a location on cam-
pus where students can work and seek support as needed. It
may be useful to provide materials for parents and families in
this resource room as well.
▶ **Accelerated learning courses:** These are courses that cover
more content at a faster pace, such as by having the course
cover two years of content in only one year.
▶ **Course offerings:** Honors classes and Advanced Placement
classes can be offered.

Student internships, magnet programs, credit by examination (i.e.,
"testing out"), and grade-skipping are also options.

For Teachers: Designing Meaningful and Motivating Units for Gifted Learners

According to Kitano and Pedersen (2002), state and Common Core
standards afford a strong curriculum framework for teaching gifted
learners. The best way to use this framework to help gifted learners is to
build upon students' background knowledge and experiences to develop
challenging and meaningful lessons and activities. This is where you
refer back to your Knowledge of Students (KOS; see Chapter 1) that is
ever-evolving to design units and/or lessons that build upon students'
schema.

**Step 1: Preassess Students' Current Understanding of Topics
Covered in the Unit.** This will help show you what, specifically, you
may need to teach within a standard and unit. It may also allow gifted
students to demonstrate mastery of a unit beforehand, which may lead

you to substitute extension activities for more rudimentary activities within a unit.

Step 2: Design Instructional Unit and Lesson Plans.

▸ Choose an instructional end goal, based on grade-level standards, that integrates real-world relevancy, is challenging but achievable with the right supports, is open-ended, piques student interests/curiosity, and includes a clear, fair rubric for evaluation.

▸ Consider how you can break down the necessary steps into bite-sized lessons to complete the end goal. Create a map or calendar for the unit that includes the necessary standards or extensions to cover throughout the unit.

Step 3: Day-to-Day Instruction of the Unit.

▸ Be open and receptive to student choice throughout the unit, including timing, task structure, and task development. This may look like a student choosing which activity within a project to start first or how long they want to work on that task before starting the next, or even coming up with new extension activities if they have shown mastery of a skill within an activity.

▸ Facilitate learning teams between students.

▸ Provide clear, timely, and actionable feedback on a regular schedule (see Table 10). You will want to schedule when you will confer or meet with each student to provide them with this feedback.

  ▹ Provide opportunities for student autonomy throughout the unit while maintaining a realistic pace.

  ▹ Support and guide students to set goals, self-monitor, and self-assess throughout the unit by guiding them to refer to unit rubrics and/or expectations.

  ▹ Scaffold student thinking with higher order thinking questions.

Step 4: Unit/Task Completion. Guide students to reflect and self-evaluate their work based on a provided rubric. A self-reflection rubric

Table 10

Providing Clear, Timely, and Actionable Feedback

	What It Is	Example	What It Lacks
Clear Feedback	Feedback that is easily understood by the recipient.	*You did a great job throwing the ball during that game; too bad your swing wasn't better.*	The feedback would have been better if it explained how to fix the problem and if it was given during the game.
Timely Feedback	Feedback that is given in time for the recipient to make adjustments.	*You need to work on your swing. Just keep your eye on the ball.*	The feedback is given in the right amount of time, but it isn't clear what about the swing was not good, nor does it teach how to fix it.
Clear and Actionable Feedback	Feedback that is given to teach the recipient how to improve in an area.	*Too bad you couldn't have had more patience during the game with your swing. Next time, you need take one breath as you see the ball leave the pitcher's hand before you start your swing.*	This is actionable feedback, but it wasn't given in time to correct the behavior during the game.
Clear, Timely, and Actionable Feedback	Feedback that is clearly explained with specific areas for improvement and in time for the recipient to make those changes.	*Hey! You're up to bat next. This time, I want you to take a breath as you see the ball leave the pitcher's hand before you start your swing. You got this!*	

can be found on this book's resource page at https://www.prufrock. com/Identifying-and-Supporting-Gifted-English-Language-Learners-Re sources.aspx.

Step 5: Postassess.

▶ Confer with students to share results and guide student reflection for continued growth in the next unit.

▶ Celebrate student success and guide discussion for continued areas of growth.

Step 6: Teacher Reflection and Data Analysis to Plan Future Lessons/Units. Reflect on the lesson, including what went well and what areas could be improved. Then, analyze what areas students may need more support with and what areas students need less support with based on newly collected data.

For Parents, Administrators, Teachers, and District/State Leaders: Asking Quality Questions to Drive Student Thinking

Imagine you are meeting someone for the first time, possibly a role model or a friend of a friend. You took the time to get ready so you can make a good first impression. You start by trying to ask questions to get to know them, but they only reply with short responses or yes/no answers. Afterward, you feel like you learned nothing about this person. So you think back to your questions: *Where are you from? What's your favorite food? Do you have siblings?* These questions seem like perfectly normal introductory questions, but they are known as closed questions, meaning that they can be answered with simple recall or memory. They also allow limited opportunities for extended discourse. Closed question responses may include yes/no answers or simple reporting of information. Open questions require a deeper and more thoughtful response, such as justifying an opinion, proving a point, or explaining one's thinking about a phenomenon. Examples of open questions may include: *What was your favorite thing about growing up in your hometown? I love trying new restaurants—what are your favorite restaurants in this area?*

Simply changing a few words in the question immediately elicits a more detailed and critical response.

In a classroom setting, considering word choice and phrasing when asking questions can be the difference between a one-word response and sparking critical thinking. How many times have you asked a question, only to get a shoulder shrug? Quality questions ensure that students must critically think about their response to avoid simple regurgitation of information. With that in mind, it is crucial for teachers to carefully develop student questioning during the lesson planning process. Creating quality questions has several advantages during the planning process, including:

- ▶ the assurance that lessons have strategic and relevant questions to guide students to reach the end goal,
- ▶ the ability to tier or scaffold questions to best meet student learning needs, and
- ▶ the removal of the pressure to generate questions during the lesson.

Quality questions are questions that (1) can illicit several acceptable answers, (2) integrate higher order thinking, and (3) require responses that include a justification. They can be easily integrated into any content area. The following sections focus on creating quality questions for literacy and math.

Literacy Questions. One way to create quality questions for literacy is using the literacy standards with the levels of knowledge from Bloom's (1956) taxonomy. Figure 23 shows what understanding should look like at each level, with remember being the lowest level and create being the highest level. The graphic shows the level of knowledge using keywords and phrases that represent how well a student knows the topic. The purpose of the taxonomy is to grow students' knowledge of a concept beyond the level of remembering toward more complex levels, such as application and creation.

Think about how you learn concepts. When you first learn something, you may be able to answer a similar question about that topic, meaning you understand the concept. But then, when you are given a question that requires you to apply your knowledge of that skill, you

Figure 23
Bloom's Taxonomy

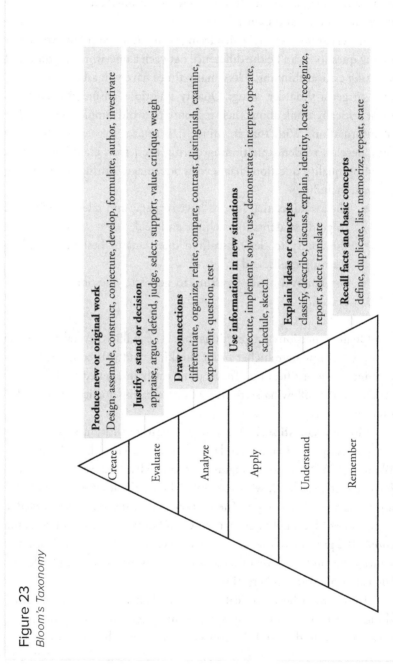

Note. This work is a derivative of "Bloom's Taxonomy," by Center for Teaching, Vanderbilt University, 2016, retrieved from https://www.flickr.com/photos/vandycft/29428436431. CC BY 2.0.

are unable. This means that you have a simple understanding of that topic but struggle with its application. Integrating Bloom's levels into the lessons, rather than saving the hardest types of questions for tests, can address these feelings of frustration and anxiety.

To help students reach higher levels of thinking within literacy using Bloom's taxonomy, follow these steps:

1. Choose a standard/topic/content area.
2. Fill in a blank version of Bloom's chart for that standard.
3. Organize the lesson or unit's activities so that students can move from one level of Bloom's to the next.

You can then use quality questions that integrate the levels of Bloom's taxonomy to create observable activities for students to complete. This process is seen in Table 11, which shows the corresponding quality questions for a text based on Bloom's, along with the activity for students to complete.

Another method for creating quality questions for literacy is using the Question-Answer Relationship (QAR; Raphael, 1982). The QAR format has four main types of questions that require the reader to look back in the book or think about their understanding of the book using their own knowledge. QAR questions support students' understanding of the relationship between a question and its answer, thus helping them to understand the question being asked. See Table 12 for examples of QAR questions.

This book's online resource page includes a QAR Sort activity to help students to better understand QAR questions and how to solve them (see https://www.prufrock.com/Identifying-and-Supporting-Gift ed-English-Language-Learners-Resources.aspx). Focusing on questions can help students to better understand how to answer them, which may be especially helpful for ELLs. After students have practiced under standing the various types of questions using a sort activity, teachers can begin offering tiered questions to build students' knowledge about the text. They can also guide students to create their own questions about the book using question stems for each of the four types of questions.

The Bloom's taxonomy approach and the QAR format offer meth ods to increase students' higher order and problem-solving skills using

Table 11

Using Bloom's Taxonomy to Create Quality Questions About a Text

	Quality Question(s)	Corresponding Activity
Remember	*What is the text about?*	Describe what happened in the book.
Understand	*What are the most important details about the text?*	Choose 2–3 quotes or facts from the text and explain why they are important.
Apply	*What can you learn from this text?*	Explain how you can use what you learned from this text in your own life.
Analyze	*What events led up to this event? What can you infer from the text?*	Create a set of pictures to show what led up to the event.
Evaluate	*What parts of the text are more important than others? Why?*	Create a diagram to show what parts of the text are more important than others and include an explanation.
Create	*What events could you add to the text that would have changed the outcome of the text? Why?*	Create 2–3 new events to add to the text that would change the outcome of the text.

a text. They both integrate various forms of questions and incorporate scaffolding for the student to be able to answer harder questions after answering more simple questions.

Math Questions. Creating quality questions for math is simple in terms of the steps and the needed language. To make quality math questions, two research-based methods, the backward planning approach and the question modification method, may be used (Sullivan & Lilburn, 2002):

- ▶ **Backward planning:**
  - ▷ Step 1: Select a topic/standard/concept.
  - ▷ Step 2: Create a closed question and then answer it.
  - ▷ Step 3: Create an open question using the answer from Step 2.

Table 12

Using QAR to Create Quality Questions About a Text

In the Book	In My Head
Right There The answer to the question is right in the text, requiring little thinking and searching. **Examples:** ▸ What did she do at her grandparents' house? ▸ Who ate all of the cookies? ▸ When did the boy get to the party? ▸ Where do lions live? ▸ What do rabbits eat? ▸ How fast can alligators run? ▸ How big can a giraffe grow to be?	**Author and Me** The answer is not directly in the text. The reader must use their background knowledge and the text to figure out the answer. **Examples:** ▸ Do you agree with her consequence for not doing her homework? ▸ How do you think they felt when they saw that he had eaten all of the cookies? ▸ Why do you think the boy was late to the party? ▸ Do you think the savannah is a good place for lions to live? Why?
Think and Search The answer is in the text but requires the reader to look in multiple places in the text to complete the question. **Examples:** ▸ What events led up to the ending? ▸ Where can different mammals live? ▸ The boy gave many excuses for being late. What were his excuses? ▸ How would you describe Sue? ▸ What did you learn about alligators?	**On My Own** The answer is not in the text. The reader must use their background knowledge to answer the question. **Examples:** ▸ What do you like to do at your grandparents' house? ▸ What are your favorite types of cookies? ▸ Where would you choose to live, and why? ▸ What animals would you like to see at the zoo? Why? ▸ When was a time when you were late? ▸ What are your favorite types of parties?

Note. The QAR method is drawn from Raphael, 1982.

Table 13
Creating Quality Math Questions

Method 1: Backward Planning Method

Step 1. Select a topic/standard/concept.	Place value
Step 2. Create a closed question and then answer it.	4$\underline{5}$2 What is the value of the underlined number?
Step 3. Create an open question using the answer from Step 2.	What do you know about the number 452?

Method 2: Modifying a Standard Question

Step 1. Select a topic/standard/concept.	Addition	Subtraction
Step 2. Choose or find standard question for that topic.	945 + 291 =	791 - 524 = 267
Step 3. Modify it to form a quality question.	While walking home in the rain, my homework got wet. Some numbers disappeared. My paper looked like this: 9 □ 5 + □ 9 1 □ 3 □	Move the numbers around so that their difference is between 200 and 300.

- ► **Modify a standard question:**
  - ▻ Step 1: Select a topic/standard/concept.
  - ▻ Step 2: Choose or find a standard question for that topic.
  - ▻ Step 3: Modify it to form a quality question.

See Table 13 for examples of both methods. Table 14 outlines other examples of quality math questions related to place value.

Quality questions can make any lesson or unit more challenging and engaging. Quality questions can also lead to greater understanding

Table 14
Quality Questions for Math: Place Value

Grades	Quality Questions
K–2	▶ What numbers can you make using 9, 2, and 0? ▶ A two-digit number contains exactly one 7. What could the number be? ▶ What numbers can you make that are below 100 and have 2 in the tens place?
3–4	▶ A number is rounded to 1600. What could the original number be? ▶ How many numbers can you make using the digits 5, 6, 7, and 8 if you can only use each digit once in each number? ▶ How many items can you find in a sales ad that have a 9 in the tenths or hundredths place?
5–6	▶ Two numbers are multiplied to equal 25,000. What can the two numbers be? ▶ What numbers can you make using 7, 9, 5, 3, 0, and 2?

of a topic, and thus greater achievement. According to Marzano et al. (2001), the types of questions that result in the greatest student gains are ones that either require students to (a) recognize similarities and differences or (b) synthesize or annotate their thinking about the text. Therefore, it is recommended that teachers and parents learn and practice forming quality questions to extend students' thinking.

Bibliotherapy: An Effective Counseling Strategy for Gifted Learners

"The best and most beautiful things in the world cannot be seen or even touched— they must be felt with the heart."

—Helen Keller

For Parents, Teachers, Administrators, and District/State Leaders

Bibliotherapy is a tool to help readers cope with personal problems through identifying with characters in a text that are similar to them (Adderholdt-Elliott & Eller, 1989). Figure 24 provides a visual of the step-by-step process that takes place during bibliotherapy.

Bibliotherapy takes place when a child selects a book and discovers characters similar to themselves. This is known as the identification process. As the child starts to notice more similarities, the connection between the child and the character becomes stronger. This connection serves as a form of catharsis as the child realizes that they are not alone in facing similar challenges in their own life. By learning about a character with similarities to them, the child gains insight into how to handle similar situations (Abellán-Pagnani & Hébert, 2012). The process of bibliotherapy can occur one-on-one, or within a whole-class context, using a fitting text. In Abellán-Pagnani and Hébert's (2012) study, one teacher asked students to share their feelings, as well as listen to others, to support students in recognizing that they all had similar feelings about the text. Bibliotherapy nurtures a sense of togetherness or camaraderie. Moreover, research has shown that bibliotherapy is a good coping strategy for (gifted) children as they are able to see how others deal with adversity in safe and nonconfrontational environments. Seeing a character in a book dealing with similar events can also help them to develop and understand their own emotions about issues that they might not have understood before (Halsted, 2009). This section explores the research behind bibliotherapy, as well as present methods for implementing bibliotherapy to support gifted ELLs grappling with various social and emotional needs.

Teachers can effectively use bibliotherapy to tackle issues such as bullying, peer pressure, or feelings of being different (Adderholdt-Elliott & Eller, 1989). By reading and discussing the situations that characters face and how they handle them, students can develop coping and anticipatory tools for handling similar problems in the future. Bibliotherapy can be particularly beneficial for gifted students because it helps them to develop social and emotional coping strategies. Exposing gifted learners

Figure 24
Stages of Bibliotherapy Process

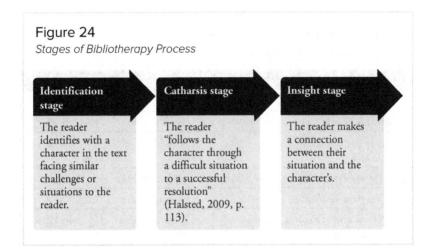

Identification stage	Catharsis stage	Insight stage
The reader identifies with a character in the text facing similar challenges or situations to the reader.	The reader "follows the character through a difficult situation to a successful resolution" (Halsted, 2009, p. 113).	The reader makes a connection between their situation and the character's.

to texts that are about gifted peer groups helps them to better understand their own challenges through the eyes of the gifted peer group in the text (Flack & Lamb, 1984). Table 15 presents a list of fictional texts about gifted learners. While implementing bibliotherapy, it is important to recognize that the final stage of insight may take some time, as students may not immediately recognize or understand the feelings of the character after the resolution or how the character's experiences correspond with their own (Shrodes, 1949).

Teachers must also carefully select texts for bibliotherapy and read the text beforehand. This way, teachers can be prepared to share their own feelings about the text as well as key discussion questions (Halsted, 2002). During the lesson(s), the teacher should guide students to be tolerant of others and respect the feelings of others (Hynes & Hynes-Berry, 1986).

Ultimately, the purpose of bibliotherapy is to guide students to cope with challenging situations or emotions that they might struggle with or not otherwise understand.

Table 15
*Texts About Gifted Learners for Developing
Social and Emotional Competence*

Text	Author	Age Range
Archibald Frisby	Michael Chesworth	5–9
Morris and Boris series	B. Wiseman	5–8
Fables ("The Crocodile in the Bedroom")	Arnold Lobel	6–12
Be a Perfect Person in Just Three Days!	Stephen Manes	8–12
The Phantom Tollbooth	Norton Juster	8–12
The Adventures of Penrose the Mathematical Cat	Theoni Pappas	9–12
A Wrinkle in Time	Madeleine L'Engle	9–13
Where Do You Think You're Going, Christopher Columbus?	Jean Fritz	9–15
The Survival Guide for Gifted Kids	Judy Galbraith	10 and under
A Gebra Named Al	Wendy Isdell	13 and up
Sophie's World: A Novel About the History of Philosophy	Jostein Gaarder	13 and up

Fostering a Growth Mindset: For Parents, Teachers, and Administrators

The purpose of a growth mindset is to move away from a fixed mindset in order to take risks, learn from mistakes, and continue to grow. A person with a growth mindset seeks to always be learning and growing. Conversely, a person with a fixed mindset accepts that there are some things they cannot do, and therefore they should not bother to try. A person with a fixed mindset also believes that it is possible to reach an ideal level of intelligence or perfection, and thus not have a need to improve anymore. Research has noted that reinforcing how bright or intelligent a child is at an early age can lead students to have a fixed mindset (Andersen & Nielsen, 2016). A student's mindset, either

Table 16

Student Phrase Comparison Between a Fixed
Mindset and a Growth Mindset

Fixed Mindset	Growth Mindset
I'm not good at this.	I am not good at this *yet!*
I hate _____!	I might like this if I work hard to become better.
This is too hard!	Practicing will make this easier.
I can't learn this.	I can learn with practice.
I am bad at _____.	I can become better at this with hard work and practice.

fixed or growth, also plays a large role in how that student perceives or approaches learning. With a fixed mindset, they may believe in finite stances such as "I'll never learn math," whereas with a growth mindset, they may change that phrase to say, "I am not good at math *yet.*" This implies that they need more chances to learn and practice to become better in math.

If parents or teachers are unaware of the dangers of a fixed mindset, they will continue to reinforce fixed concepts with phrases such as "You are so smart," "You are great at math," or "You are the best piano player." However, Andersen and Nielsen (2016) found that instruction with a growth mindset approach resulted in large academic gains in literacy achievement. The strongest gains were in students whose parents had a more fixed mindset prior to the literacy instruction. This shows that a student can move away from a fixed mindset toward a growth mindset to make greater academic gains. Table 16 presents a comparison of student phrases from a fixed mindset point of view compared to a growth mindset point of view.

The key to promoting a growth mindset is to praise the effort rather than the product. The effort is the amount of work that goes into learning or achieving success, whereas the product is the end result achieved. Praising the effort reinforces a growth mindset to always be working to achieve more or better. On the other hand, praises such as "You're so smart" teach the learner that only intelligence is valued, thus fostering a fixed mindset. Additionally, these phrases teach the learner that everything should be easy for them because they are "so smart." To prevent or correct a fixed mindset you can: (1) change your phrasing, (2) practice growth mindset activities with the student, and (3) read growth mindset books. This section explores these three ways to adopt a growth mindset.

Change Your Phrasing

> "No matter what people tell you, words and ideas change the world."
>
> —Robin Williams

Similar to quality questions, you can make or break a mindset with your choice of words or how you arrange those words. "You're so smart" reinforces the fixed mindset belief that intelligence is the ultimate goal, and a student may fear that if they struggle or fail, then they will not be considered intelligent. These kinds of phrases can also lead to fears of failure, risk aversion, fears of not being able to live up to others' expectations, and perfectionism. The phrase "You're so smart" was not intended to cause these negative thoughts, but from a child's perspective some of these fears about failure and perfection seem very logical. Parents, teachers, and administrators need to become knowledgeable about how to change their word choice to foster growth mindsets. But how do you change a fixed mindset phrase to a growth mindset phrase? The answer is to stress the importance of work or effort. A fixed mindset celebrates or criticizes the final product or outcome, whereas a growth mindset celebrates the process of growing and practicing. Highlighting the student's work process teaches them the importance of hard work rather than reinforcing concepts of instant gratification. Table 17 provides examples of phrases that foster growth mindsets, both for praise and critique.

Students need to understand that hard work is a part of that journey and not just the destination. This is especially true for gifted ELLs, as they may not understand or see the work that other students put in to become successful within a content area or hobby. The gifted ELL may see a fantastic artist, great musician, or superb mathematician and

Table 17

Phrases to Foster a Growth Mindset (Brock & Hundley, 2018)

Praise	
Product (Fixed Mindset)	**Process (Growth Mindset)**
You're so smart.	I like how you looked back in the book for the answer.
You are fantastic in math.	You worked so hard to solve that problem.
You're a genius at writing.	Your writing is very organized and clearly thought out.

Critique	
Person (Fixed Mindset)	**Process (Growth Mindset)**
Maybe tennis isn't for you.	Keep practicing! You get better every time you practice.
How could you do this? This was a huge mistake!	That didn't seem to go well. What could you do differently next time?
Your best just wasn't good enough.	You didn't reach your goal yet, but what have you learned?

naturally think, "Wow, I will never be that good." In this example, the gifted ELL needs to learn about how a person practiced to become great at a certain skill. The same is true for younger students learning in the classroom. Many of my former students have said to me over the years, "Learning the alphabet was so easy." But then I correct them and explain, "It was not always easy for you. I remember teaching you the alphabet for several months before you knew all of your letters and sounds correctly, but you have forgotten that, so now the alphabet seems easy. The same is true when you learn something new. Everything seems hard until you are able to do it, and then it becomes easy." The goal of a growth mindset is to remove the focus from the words *easy* and *hard*, and to transition the focus to students' description of their work or effort to learn that skill. One way to do this is to guide students to reflect upon how they learned with questions like:

► How were you at _____ in the beginning?
► How did you become better at _____?

▶ What else can you do to continue getting better at _____?

These reflective questions and phrasing choices guide the student to recognize their hard work to achieve their goal. This will help them to understand over time that they can achieve a lot more with hard work.

Growth Mindset Activities

"Tell me and I'll forget, show me and I may remember. Involve me and I will learn."

—Benjamin Franklin

Adjusting phrasing and word choice is a great first step toward a growth mindset. However, just as Benjamin Franklin said, learners need opportunities to practice a skill to truly learn it. The following is a list of activities that you can easily implement into your classroom to form and foster a growth mindset. Each of these activities will need to be guided using direct instruction, with which the teacher introduces the activity, explains the purpose, and provides time for practice so that students can take ownership when working independently.

▶ **Create a growth mindset motto, mantra, or catchphrase:** Creating a motto or mantra can help students to focus positively to keep working hard when learning becomes tough. Some examples may include: "I've got this," "No pain, no gain," or "Just keep swimming."

▶ **Draw your fixed mindset:** Have students create a drawing of their fixed mindset, including their negative self-talk. This activity can help students to recognize their fixed mindset to better control it. Sometimes we do not realize that we have negative self-talk about ourselves until someone else brings it to our attention.

▶ **Create accountability partners:** Divide the class into teams of two. The partners will become accountability partners who serve as one another's cheerleaders. For example, if and when one of them is struggling to complete a task or activity due to negative, fixed mindset thinking, the accountability partner can help them to change their mindset.

- ▶ **Name your fixed mindset:** This can help students to recognize their negative thoughts. When the negative fixed mindset thoughts start to become too loud, students can say "Back off, _____," or "No way, _____," to reinforce positive self-talk.
- ▶ **Practice mindset skits:** Prepare students to cope with negative self-talk through skits and role-playing in which one student has a fixed mindset while the other tries to teach them how to change to a growth mindset. By practicing the process before they hit an obstacle, they can learn what to do when they actually run into difficulty (Brock & Hundley, 2018).

Teachers should explain and teach what self-talk is, so that students can understand this inner voice. For examples on how to teach self-talk, refer to the Growth Mindset Lesson located in Appendix C. Another activity to tackle negative or fixed mindset talk is to place students in teams of two and present them with a famous growth mindset quote. The team of two must read their quote and explain how it relates to a growth mindset. Famous quotes might include:

- ▶ "If you hear a voice within you say, 'you cannot paint' then by all means paint, and that voice will be silenced."—Vincent van Gogh
- ▶ "Nothing is impossible. The word itself says, 'I'm possible!'"—Audrey Hepburn
- ▶ "It is hard to fail, but it is worse never to have tried to succeed."—Theodore Roosevelt
- ▶ "I can accept failure, everyone fails at something. But I can't accept not trying."—Michael Jordan
- ▶ "Twenty years from now you will be more disappointed by the things that you didn't do than by the ones you did do. So sail away from the safe harbor. Explore. Dream. Discover."—Mark Twain

Afterward, partners can share with others using a conga line strategy. This strategy involves dividing the partners into two rows, so that one partner is on one side and the other is on the other side, facing each other. Then you can play music (optional) while one row stands still and the other row moves one person down so that each student is now standing in front of a new partner. During the conga line strategy, each person will take turns sharing their team's quote and how it relates to a growth mindset. I usually assign which side will go first and set a timer to make sure that students keep talking the whole time, instead of saying a quick line and then stopping. It is crucial for ELLs to be able to practice communicating to develop their oral language skills. Then, when the timer goes off, I set another timer for the other partner to share. I rotate between the partners to listen in on their conversations, but I never add or say anything. After the timer goes off, I talk about partners who did a great job and why. Some comments might include, "I loved how Vy talked the whole time with her partner," or "Josué did a great job of asking questions to get Josias to keep talking when the timer hadn't gone off yet." This teaches students that I am actively listening to see who is working hard so that they continue to stay on task. To encourage students to keep talking, I ask partners to ask each other questions about what they shared to promote active listening. Additionally, after I have taught and practiced the conga line strategy a few times, I let the students share what their partner did well and what they could work on. This builds upon active listening and makes the speaker feel good because their partner celebrates what they did well.

The goal of the conga line activity for famous growth mindset quotes is to teach students how to turn fixed mindset talk into growth mindset talk. For especially struggling thinkers, you can also use the "if/then goal-setting strategy." Here, you help the student to choose a goal and use that goal to create an if/then sentence. For example:

- Goal: *To know what to do.* If/then sentence: "If I don't know what to do, then I will ask a friend for help."
- Goal: *To learn how to* _____. If/then sentence: "If I do not master _____, then I will practice for 20 minutes every night."
- Goal: *To pass a test.* If/then sentence: "If I do not pass my test, then I will study the questions I missed to do better next time."

The growth mindset activities presented are an excellent next step in supporting students struggling with a fixed mindset or negative self-talk. They allow students to practice using growth mindset phrases so that they can internalize growth self-talk. The activities also help students to know what to do when they start having negative or fixed mindset self-talk, which is an essential skill. Often, students can recognize the problem but are not sure how to fix it. Growth mindset activities afford students a toolkit to deal with that situation.

Multicultural Growth Mindset Books

> "Unless we learn to know ourselves, we run the danger of destroying ourselves."
>
> —Ja A. Jahannes

Another step to fostering a growth mindset for gifted ELLs is to read multicultural books that include characters from varied backgrounds and cultures and are written by authors with varied backgrounds. The defining characteristic of a multicultural book is that it does not promote negative stereotypes and instead celebrates diversity. Using a variety of multicultural books is critical because "no single piece of literature can represent a cultural group," thus raising the need to read multiple multicultural books to help students learn about various cultures (Ford et al., 2018, p. 55). It is especially important for underrepresented learners to read about characters that look like them so that they feel welcome, accepted, and celebrated. Books such as these may be called "mirror books" because students see themselves reflected in the book (Bishop, 1991). Additionally, reading multicultural books can help students to identify and form cultural connections through characters, similar to bibliotherapy, which can help them to better understand their own heritage (Radin, 2015). There is extensive research on the importance of reading multicultural books and its benefits, but what are some multicultural books that promote a growth mindset?

Table 18

Multicultural Books to Develop a Growth Mindset

Book	Author	Grade Level
Whistle for Willie	Ezra Jack Keats	K–2
Nadia, the Girl Who Couldn't Sit Still	Karlin Gray	K–3
The OK Book	Amy Krouse Rosenthal	K–3
What Do You Do With a Problem?	Kobi Yamada	1–3
What Do You Do With an Idea?	Kobi Yamada	1–3
Hana Hashimoto, Sixth Violin	Chieri Uegaki	2–5
Salt in His Shoes	Deloris Jordan	3–5

Table 18 presents a list of texts and their corresponding grade levels for students to read as a group or for the teacher to read aloud. If teachers choose to read the text aloud, any of these books can be used to implement bibliotherapy and to coach students struggling with a fixed mindset or with feelings of being an outsider. The teacher can also highlight the characters' diversity to help students to feel proud about their own diversity.

Prior to reading the book aloud, or asking students to read the text, teachers should create quality questions about the book to guide students' thinking and reflection. Some quality questions to promote a growth mindset for these books may include:

- ▸ Is there a character that you relate to in this text? How?
- ▸ How did the character solve the problem in the book? What steps were the most important for them to solve the problem? Why?
- ▸ What lesson could you learn from this book that could help you in the future?
- ▸ How did this character show that they had a growth mindset?

These questions can be discussed with partners, teams, or as a whole class, depending on the needs of the students. The purpose of these questions is for students to recognize their similarities with these characters and to learn strategies to help themselves when they feel like a task is too hard. By seeing how other characters use growth mindset strategies to achieve their goal, readers can learn how to cope in a similar situation in the future.

The methods for fostering a growth mindset presented in this section require explicit instruction and consistent reinforcement. Developing a growth mindset does not happen overnight, nor is it a lesson that you can teach in August or September and then forget for the rest of the year. As teachers, parents, and community members, it is imperative that you are consistently seeking ways to reinforce a growth mindset in your learners. This can be done through word choice, activities, and books to help learners know what to do when the "going gets tough." Will your learners give up, or will they become tough and keep going? When students hit a roadblock, will they give up because they have accepted the fixed mindset, or will they think harder to come up with another option? Consistent and ongoing positive reinforcement are required to help learners become growth-oriented, even into adulthood, as their problems become more and more complex. Therefore, it is best to start developing a growth mindset from an early age to encourage exploration, risk-taking, and failure. Ultimately, it is how you fail that determines what kind of person you will be.

Chapter Summary

Promoting and protecting students' self-esteem and cultural identity is essential in all school programs, especially in gifted programs. Many gifted ELLs feel isolated from, and in some cases inferior to, others within the gifted program because they may be the only CLED student or one of just a handful. Therefore, it is crucial for teachers to teach gifted ELLs to cope with their varied socioemotional needs using an equally varied approach. This chapter focused on how to teach gifted ELLs to accommodate their varied socioemotional needs to keep them healthy, safe, actively engaged, challenged, and supported. It presented ways parents can support their learners with enrichment, extracurricular activities, and schooling options; explored various teaching strategies, including lesson planning; taught all key players how to form quality questions to engage and challenge learners; and covered the importance of bibliotherapy and a growth mindset. Growing research suggests that students cannot learn in settings where they do not feel safe, where their physical needs have not been met, or where they are not being challenged. This is why the varied approach presented in this chapter is so important.

Discussion Questions

1. How do you support the needs of the whole child in your classroom or school?
2. What are the socioemotional needs of your students?
3. How are you continuing to inform and educate the parents of your gifted ELLs to support their learning outside of school?
4. How can you use bibliotherapy in your classroom or school?
5. How can you support your gifted ELL families to learn and use growth mindset phrases at home?

Conclusion
The Ongoing Process of Identifying and Supporting Gifted ELLs

"The fact that societies are becoming increasingly multi-ethnic, multicultural, and multi-religious is good. Diversity is a strength, not a weakness."

—António Guterres

At this point, you have learned much of what you can to increase the number of identified gifted ELLs in gifted programs, inevitably resulting in some gifted ELLs becoming identified while also leaving other potentially gifted ELLs unidentified. So, what do you do now to continue the work of increasing the number of identified gifted ELLs getting into gifted programs? This conclusion explores the "power of yet" to identify potentially gifted ELLs in their continued educational journey. Also discussed is broadening gifted ELLs' horizons with information related to immigrants who have achieved greatness.

The Power of Yet

"We cannot seek achievement for ourselves and forget about progress and prosperity for our community. . . . Our ambitions must be broad enough to include the aspirations and needs of others, for their sakes and for our own."

—Cesar Chavez

Potentially gifted ELLs may not be caught, even in the widest net, depending on a number of factors, such as transience, improper testing, misuse of evaluative criteria, and teacher apathy. Every year, I hear about a student who transitions to another school, resulting in them not being identified or struggling to become properly identified. Maybe the staff members at the new school do not know about the student's testing history or were too overwhelmed to test the student after they had missed the screening window during the move. Maybe the student's former or current ELL or AIG teacher is not knowledgeable about how to advocate for a gifted ELL. Or maybe the gifted ELL was close to identification but just not quite there. These factors can leave many gifted ELLs unidentified. However, that doesn't mean that the talent is not there or that they do not need additional support. This brings us to the "power of yet," the belief that even if a child has not demonstrated gifts and talents in an assessed area, they still may be gifted. The power of yet works to build upon growth mindset thinking and provide ongoing opportunities for students to become eligible for gifted programs.

It is important for districts and states to offer additional opportunities for underrepresented student populations to enter gifted programs. These can include additional screening opportunities, student referrals, or portfolio opportunities for potentially gifted students in grade levels after the initial screening. They can also include informal observations, work samples, and any of the other criteria outlined in Chapter 4 regarding the identification process. Offering ongoing opportunities for gifted identification ensures equitable access for all learners, especially the most vulnerable ones. Many times, gifted ELLs are tested for gifted programs when they have only been in the country for a year or less. The school, district, or program may or may not have provided the assessment in the student's home language, and the student may be ill prepared for the identification process because of their limited schooling experience in the U.S. Some districts recognize the need to provide equitable opportunities for ongoing identification and have been incorporating these best practices into their districts' gifted programs. Offering identification opportunities beyond the traditional testing window allows ELLs to be tested in later years when they are more acclimated to U.S. testing procedures, have a firmer grasp of the language demands, and have opportunities to excel academically. Without these additional opportunities for identification, many ELLs will go unidentified and ineligible for gifted programs. Several school districts are leading the way in offering these opportunities.

Successful Districts Offering Additional Opportunities for Identification

Some districts across the country are already integrating the power of yet to provide ongoing screening to identify underrepresented populations. These include Arlington Public Schools in Virginia, Palm Beach County in Florida, San Diego Unified School District in California, and Denver Public School System in Colorado. All of these districts offer additional opportunities for students to be referred for gifted program identification:

> ► **Arlington Public Schools, VA:** Arlington offers gifted identification in two areas: specific academic aptitude (math, science, English, social studies) for grades K–12 and visual and/or performing arts aptitude for grades 3–12. The district provides a universal screener for all second and fourth graders for identification. All second graders take the Naglieri Nonverbal Abilities Test in the fall, and all fourth graders take the CogAT in the fall. Students may enter the eligibility pool either through the results on the screener exam or through the referral process.

Teachers, parents, family members, or the student themselves may also make referrals. The form for referral is also provided in various languages to support underrepresented populations. Additionally, a student may be referred for gifted identification consideration at any point during their education journey, which is reviewed annually. Arlington also considers students using a multiple-criteria approach including assessments, student work samples, student interview, checklist, parent feedback, normed assessments, and any other reliable measures (Arlington Public Schools, 2017).

▸ **The School District of Palm Beach County, FL:** Palm Beach County universally screens all second-grade students for gifted eligibility using the CogAT nonverbal assessment. Students may also be referred for gifted screening by a parent/guardian, a teacher or other staff member, the student, or anyone with knowledge of the student. Students can be eligible for gifted education through two outlined methods, known as Plan A and Plan B. Plan A requires students to (1) display a majority of the characteristics of giftedness on the Gifted Characteristic Checklist Form and (2) score a 130 or higher on an individually administered IQ test. Plan B is applicable only to underrepresented student populations, such as ELLs and students from low-SES backgrounds. There are five criteria for students to become eligible for a gifted program under Plan B: (1) a combined or nonverbal score of 112 or higher on an intellectual assessment; (2) individual academic achievement on tests, such as the Kaufman Test of Educational Achievement, the Wechsler Individual Achievement Test, or the Woodcock-Johnson Tests of Achievement; (3) classroom performance, such as progress reports; (4) student score on the Gifted Characteristic Checklist for Underrepresented Populations; and (5) student portfolio, which is evaluated with an ELL representative (McCormick & Marshall, n.d.).

▸ **San Diego Unified School District, CA:** San Diego uses the acronym GATE (Gifted and Talented Education) to refer to its current program model. The San Diego GATE plan provides that all second-grade students are universally screened using the CogAT and that students in third, fourth, and fifth grade may retake or take for the first time the CogAT, based on district set criteria. In 2009, this district implemented a pilot program to identify students in grades 6–12. GATE also uses an eligibility matrix that takes into consideration students who are transient or English learning, who face socioeconomic challenges, and who have disabilities. Parents may also appeal decisions for student identification into the gifted program (Rea, 2015).

▶ **Denver Public Schools, CO:** Denver offers identification in three areas, including (1) academic aptitude (math, reading, science, social studies, writing, and world language), (2) specific talent aptitude (visual or performing arts, dance, music, psychomotor, creative or productive thinking, and/or leadership abilities), and (3) general or specific intellectual aptitude. The district provides screening for all kindergarteners, second graders, and sixth graders, using the Naglieri Nonverbal Abilities Test-3. The district also directs teachers to collect a "body of evidence" throughout the school year for students who meet outlined criteria, which is later discussed by a review committee to determine the students' eligibility. Denver also accepts referrals from anyone who knows the child to be considered for specific talent aptitude. The program stresses that gifted identification is open and accessible to all students by offering an ongoing identification process, multiple areas for identification, usage of a nonverbal assessment, committee review, and open referrals (Denver Public Schools, n.d.).

Although these programs are innovative in the area of supporting underrepresented populations, such as ELLs, there is still an ongoing need for improvement. District and state leaders should consider their own gifted program plans to look for methods to provide ongoing identification opportunities for underrepresented populations. The culture of advocacy does not stop or end after the initial identification. All key players must continue to support, plan, listen, act, and teach to advocate for the identification of gifted ELLs. By continuing the culture of advocacy, we can support the many gifted ELLs who are currently falling through the cracks.

Broadening Gifted ELLs' Horizons

> "People are like dirt. They can either nourish you and help you grow as a person or they can stunt your growth and make you wilt and die."
>
> —Plato

You may now have a number of identified gifted ELLs who are actively engaged and supported in their learning process. It is a common misconception that giftedness only refers to children; this is far from the truth. Children who are identified as gifted continue to be gifted into adulthood. The same talents that were observed in early education continue to develop or, in some cases, wither or crumble if not supported correctly. A great way to offer continued motivation for gifted ELLs is to introduce them to famous gifted ELLs who have made significant contributions to society. The following is a list of gifted individuals with various cultural backgrounds who have made significant contributions to society.

This list of impressive and impactful immigrants is intended to inspire gifted ELLs to see that people like them can achieve greatness in today's society. Parents, teachers, and administrators can help gifted ELLs to feel not only welcome in gifted programs, but also empowered through immigrants with whom they can identify.

Famous Gifted Hispanic Americans

- ▶ **Helen Rodriguez-Trias (1929–2001):** Rodriguez-Trias was born July 7, 1929, in New York City, NY. She grew up in Puerto Rico and New York, and graduated from the University of Puerto Rico in 1957, where she became an activist on issues of freedom of speech and independence. In 1960, she received her medical degree. In 1970, she became a pediatrician in New York in low-income communities and offered medical care to underprivileged children. Over the years, she has advocated for women's health rights and children's medical rights. In 2001, she received a presidential medal for her work with children, women, people with HIV/AIDS, and low-income populations (U.S. National Library of Medicine, 2015).

- ▶ **Mario Molina (1943–present):** Molina was born March 19, 1943, in Mexico City, Mexico. In 1965, Molina graduated with a Bachelor of Science degree in chemical engineering from the National Autonomous University of Mexico. He later studied at the University of California, Berkley, where he earned his Ph.D. in 1972. He has made notable contributions within the field of science, specifically regarding environmental gases. In 1995, Molina was awarded the Nobel Prize for Chemistry, along with F. Sherwood Rowland and Paul Crutzen, for research on the decomposition of the ozone. In 2013, he was awarded the U.S. Presidential Medal of Freedom (Editors of Encyclopedia Britannica, n.d.-b).

- ▶ **Jaime Escalante (1930–2010):** Escalante was born December 31, 1930, in La Paz, Bolivia. He moved to the U.S. in the 1960s and settled in Los Angeles. He began teaching math to students within a school area known for drugs and violence. Escalante became known for his ability to help students who had been deemed "unteachable" by others to pass the Advanced Placement calculus test. In 1988, he was recognized for his laudable teaching abilities in the book *Escalante: The Best Teacher in America.* The same year, a film was released about his passion for teaching and achievement entitled *Stand and Deliver* (Bio graphy.com Editors, 2019).

Famous Gifted Asian Americans

- ▶ **Katherine Luzuriaga:** Born in Bacolod, Philippines, Luzuriaga attended the Massachusetts Institute of Technology (MIT), where she earned her bachelor's and master's degrees. She later pursued her medical degree at Tufts University. Since 2012, Luzuriaga has served as the Director of the UMass Center for Clinical and Transnational Science. In 2013, she was recognized in *Time Magazine* as one of the 100 most influential people in the world. She has been recognized for her notable research of pediatric HIV/AIDS and the transmission of HIV from pregnant women to their babies during birth (University of Massachusetts Medical School, 2013).

▸ **Haing S. Ngor (1940–1996):** Born March 22, 1940, in the Bati district of Cambodia, Ngor is most well-known as a physician, actor, and activist for Cambodian refugees. He survived the Khmer Rouge takeover of Cambodia in 1975 by pretending to be a taxi driver. Because he was a physician, he was forced to hide his professional background for fear of execution. In 1979, he escaped to Thailand, and in 1980, he moved to the U.S. Ngor worked in Los Angeles as a job counselor for refugees. He was later chosen to act in the film *The Killing Fields*, for which he later received an Academy Award for his portrayal of Dith Pran. He appeared in other films and went on to advocate for Cambodian refugees. He was killed in an armed robbery in 1996 (Editors of Encyclopedia Britannica, n.d.-a).

▸ **Chi Cheng Huang (1971–present):** Born in 1971 in Columbia, SC, to Taiwanese immigrants, Huang lived in poverty for most of his upbringing. His family moved to Texas when he was in second grade. His childhood experiences with poverty made him want to help other children like himself. Throughout high school, Huang worked very hard to earn credits toward a college degree from Texas A&M. In 1993, he graduated with a bachelor's degree from there. He then attended Harvard's Medical School, where he graduated in 1997. At the age of 26, Huang wanted a break from academics and also wanted to feed his passion to help children. He decided to go to Bolivia on a missionary trip to help children from low-income areas in need of medical assistance. He took to the streets of La Paz to help orphaned and homeless children who had been victims of trauma and abuse. He helped children with various medical needs, such as tooth infection, STDs, and broken bones. Huang deeply cared for the estimated 3,000 homeless children living on the streets of La Paz. He went on to found Kaya Children International, also known as the Bolivian Street Children Project, a nonprofit organization to offer homeless children a transitional home. The organization has raised enough money to build three homes to care for the children of La Paz. Huang is currently the Executive Medical Director of General Medicine and Hospital Medicine Shared Services at Wake Forest Baptist Health System (Jones, 2017).

Famous Gifted Black American Immigrants

- ▶ **Guetty Felin:** Born in Haiti, Felin attended Queen's College in New York from 1983 to 1987, where she earned a bachelor of arts degree in communications and political science, as well as a minor in film. From 2002 to 2004, Felin served as a Film Series Curator at New York University. Since 2007, she has been a writer, director, and producer of various film projects. Felin wrote, directed, and produced the award-winning documentary *Broken Stones* about the recovery in Haiti after the devastating earthquake. She has worked on several pieces that focus on African American cultural identity, and her works have been featured in film festivals across the world (Focus on French Cinema, n.d.).

- ▶ **Chimamanda Ngozi Adichie (1977–present):** Born September 15, 1977, in Enugu, Nigeria, Adichie grew up in Nigeria and moved to the U.S. in 1997 to study at Eastern Connecticut State University. In 2001, she graduated with a bachelor's degree in communications and political science. She later earned a master's degree in creative writing from Johns Hopkins University and studied African history at Yale University. She has authored several award-winning short stories and novels. Her second novel, *Half of a Yellow Sun*, tells a historical fiction narrative of the Nigeria-Biafra War that resulted in the displacement and death of thousands of people. This book became an international best seller and was awarded the Orange Broadband Prize for Fiction in 2007. Adichie has continued to release critically acclaimed literary pieces and was a featured speaker at a TEDx Talk in 2012 (Leubering, 2020).

▶ **Ilhan Omar (1982–present):** Born October 4, 1982, in Mogadishu, Somalia, Omar fled from Somalia's civil war at the age of 8 with her family. They survived in a refugee camp in Kenya for 4 years before moving to Minneapolis in 1997. At the age of 14, she helped as an interpreter for her grandfather at local Democratic–Farmer–Labor Party caucuses. She earned a bachelor's degree in political science and international studies from North Dakota State University in 2011. In 2016, Omar became the first Somali-American, Muslim legislator in the U.S. In 2019, Omar began serving as the U.S. Representative for Minnesota's 5th Congressional District (Ilhan for Congress, n.d.).

Similar to the mirror books, these examples can help students to see themselves in opportunities and positions of greatness. These examples can be introduced to students using a jigsaw teaching strategy, which allows every student to become an expert on something that they will later teach to other teams. First, students are put into teams that are assigned a famous person. Then, as a team, they will read and discuss their person. Next, each team member must record a description or create a visual for their team's assigned person. Afterward, students will be dispersed to new teams so that each new team consists of one member from each of the original teams. Within their new teams, members will teach each other about their impressive and impactful immigrants. It may be helpful to offer students a graphic organizer to record their team's information and to record what they learn about the other individuals. The purpose of this activity is to get students listening, speaking, reading, and writing about individuals that look like them and to inspire their dreams for the future. Activities such as this can help show gifted ELLs that they have a purpose and that gifted programs can be the vehicle to help them reach their future dreams.

Nurturing gifts and talents is a common thread throughout the previous the chapters. It is what allows students to grow academically and to develop new or existing talents. Gifts and talents in ELLs especially need to be nurtured by key players for them to even gain entry to the gifted playing field. There is still a high need for improvement for the identification of gifted ELLs into gifted programs. The topics covered in this book can serve as a starting point for key players to make changes at the grassroots level.

Discussion Questions

1. What is the "power of yet," and how can you use it?
2. What are your next steps in the process of identifying and supporting gifted ELLs?
3. Why must identifying and supporting gifted ELLs be an ongoing process?
4. How can the changes that you make guide this process?

References

Abellán-Pagnani, L., & Hébert, T. P. (2012). Using picture books to guide and inspire young gifted Hispanic students. *Gifted Child Today, 36*(1), 47–56. https://doi.org/10.1177/1076217512459735

Adams, C. M., & Chandler, K. L. (Eds.). (2014). *Effective program models for gifted students from underserved populations.* Prufrock Press.

Adderholdt-Elliott, M., & Eller, S. H. (1989). Counseling students who are gifted through bibliotherapy. *TEACHING Exceptional Children, 22*(1), 26–31. https://doi.org/10.1177/004005998902200106

Aguirre, N. (2003). ESL students in gifted education. In J. A. Castellano (Ed.), *Special populations in gifted education: Working with diverse gifted learners* (pp. 17–34). Pearson.

Alvino, J., McDonnel, R. C., & Richert, S. (1981). National survey of identification practices in gifted and talented education. *Exceptional Children, 48*(2), 124–132. https://doi.org/10.1177/001440298104800205

Andersen, S. C., & Nielsen, H. S. (2016). Reading intervention with a growth mindset approach improves children's skills. *Proceedings of the National Academy of Sciences, 113*(43), 12111–12113. https://doi.org/10.1073/pnas.1607946113

Arlington Public Schools. (2017). *Arlington public schools local plan for the education of the gifted: 2017–2022.* https://www.apsva.us/wp-content/uploads/2018/03/Final-Local-Plan-for-Website-2017-2022.pdf

Armour-Thomas, E. (1992). Intellectual assessment of children from culturally diverse backgrounds. *School Psychology Review, 21*(4), 552–565.

Ball, W. H., & Brewer, P. (2000). *Socratic seminars in the block.* Eye on Education.

Bianco, M., & Harris, B. (2014). Strength-based RTI: Developing gifted potential in Spanish-speaking English language learners. *Gifted Child Today, 37*(3), 169–176. https://doi.org/10.1177/1076217514530115

Biography.com Editors. (2019). *Jaime Escalante biography.* https://www.biography.com/scholar/jaime-escalante

Bishop, R. S. (1990). Mirrors, windows, and sliding glass doors. *Perspectives: Choosing and Using Books for the Classroom, 6*(3).

Bloom, B. (Ed.). (1956). *Taxonomy of educational objectives: The classification of educational goals. Handbook I: Cognitive domain.* Longmans Green.

Brock, A., & Hundley, H. (2018). *In other words: Phrases for growth mindset: A teachers guide to empowering students through effective praise and feedback.* Ulysses Press.

Brown, J., & Pamintuan, M. (2010). *Flat Stanley.* HarperCollins.

Castellano, J. A. (1998). *Identifying and assessing gifted and talented bilingual Hispanic students* (ED423104). ERIC. https://files.eric.ed.gov/fulltext/ED423104.pdf

Castellano, J. A. (2002). Renavigating the waters: The identification and assessment of culturally and linguistically diverse students for gifted and talented education. In J. A. Castellano & E. Diaz (Eds.), *Reaching new horizons: Gifted and talented education for culturally and linguistically diverse students* (pp. 94–116). Allyn & Bacon.

Castellano, J. A. (2003). *Special populations in gifted education: Working with diverse gifted learners.* Allyn & Bacon.

Center for Learning, Vanderbilt University. (2016). *Bloom's taxonomy.* https://www.flickr.com/photos/vandycft/29428436431

Charlotte-Mecklenburg Schools. (n.d.). *Gifted identification*. https://www. cms.k12.nc.us/cmsdepartments/ci/astd/Pages/Gateway.aspx

Cline, S., & Schwartz, D. (1999). *Diverse populations of gifted children: Meeting their needs in the regular classroom and beyond*. Merrill.

Coleman, L. J., & Cross, T. L. (2005). *Being gifted in school: An introduction to development, guidance, and teaching* (2nd ed.). Prufrock Press.

Cross, J. R., & Dockery, D. D. (2014). *Identification of low-income gifted learners: A review of recent research*. Jack Kent Cooke Foundation.

Denver Public Schools. (n.d.). *Identification process*. https://studentequity. dpsk12.org/gifted-talented/assessment-and-identification-process

Diaz, E. (2002). Framing an historical context for the evaluation of culturally and linguistically diverse students with gifted potential: 1850s to 1980s. In J. A. Castellano & E. Diaz (Eds.), *Reaching new horizons: Gifted and talented education for culturally and linguistically diverse students* (pp. 1–28). Allyn & Bacon.

Diaz, R. M., & Klingler, C. (1991). Toward an exploratory model of the interaction between bilingualism and cognitive development. In E. Bialystok (Ed.), *Language processing in bilingual children* (pp. 167–192). Cambridge University Press.

Editors of Encyclopedia Britannica. (n.d.-a). *Haing S. Ngor: Cambodian physician and actor*. https://www.britannica.com/biography/Haing-S-Ngor

Editors of Encyclopedia Britannica. (n.d.-b). *Mario Molina: American chemist*. https://www.britannica.com/biography/Mario-Molina

Encyclopedia of World Biography. (n.d.). *Alexander Graham Bell biography*. https://www.notablebiographies.com/Ba-Be/Bell-Alexander-Graham.html

Ennis, S. R., Rios-Vargas, M., & Albert, N. G. (2011, May). *The Hispanic population: 2010*. U.S. Census Bureau. https://www.census.gov/prod/ cen2010/briefs/c2010br-04.pdf

Esquierdo, J. J. (2006). *Early identification of Hispanic English language learners for gifted and talented programs* [Doctoral dissertation, Texas A&M University]. OAKTrust. https://hdl.handle.net/1969.1/3944

Every Student Succeeds Act, 20 U.S.C. § 6301 (2015). https://congress. gov/114/plaws/publ95/PLAW-114publ95.pdf

Flack, J. D., & Lamb, P. (1984). Making use of gifted characters in literature. *Gifted Child Today, 7*(5), 3–11. https://doi.org/10.1177/107621758400700501

Focus on French Cinema. (n.d.). *Guetty Felin.* https://focusonfrenchcinema.com/guetty-felin

Ford, D. Y. (2011). *Multicultural gifted education* (2nd ed.). Prufrock Press.

Ford, D. Y. (2013). *Recruiting and retaining culturally different students in gifted education.* Prufrock Press.

Ford, D. Y., & Grantham, T. C. (2003). Providing access for culturally diverse gifted students: From deficit thinking to dynamic thinking. *Theory Into Practice, 42*(3), 217–225. https://doi.org/10.1207/s15430421tip4203_8

Ford, D. Y., Walters, N. M., Byrd, J. A., & Harris, B. N. (2018). I want to read about me: Engaging and empowering gifted black girls using multicultural literature and bibliotherapy. *Gifted Child Today, 42*(1), 53–57. https://doi.org/10.1177/1076217518804851

Frasier, M. M., & Passow, A. H. (1994). *Toward a new paradigm for identifying talent potential* (RM94112). University of Connecticut, National Research Center on the Gifted and Talented.

Freehill, M. F. (1961). *Gifted children: Their psychology and education.* Macmillan.

Gardner, H. (2011). *Frames of mind: The theory of multiple intelligences.* Basic Books. (Original work published 1983)

Genesee, F. (Ed.). (2011). *Educating second language children: The whole child, the whole curriculum, the whole community.* Cambridge University Press.

Gentry, M., Fugate, C. M., Wu, J., & Castellano, J. A. (2014). Gifted Native American students: Literature, lessons, and future directions. *Gifted Child Quarterly, 58*(2), 98–110. https://doi.org/10.1177/0016986214521660

Gershon, L. (2015). *A short history of standardized test.* JSTOR Daily. https://daily.jstor.org/short-history-standardized-tests

Gersten, R., & Baker, S. (2000). What we know about effective instructional practices for English-language learners. *Exceptional Children, 66*(4), 454–470. https://doi.org/10.1177/001440290006600402

Gonzalez, A. (2016). *10 assumptions to rethink about English-language learners*. Education Week Teacher. https://www.edweek.org/tm/arti cles/2016/11/01/10-assumptions-to-rethink-about-english-lang uage-learners.html

Granada, A. J. (2002). Addressing the curriculum, instruction, and assessment needs of the gifted bilingual/bicultural student. In J. A. Castellano & E. Diaz (Eds.), *Reaching new horizons: Gifted and talented education for culturally and linguistically diverse students* (pp. 133–153). Allyn & Bacon.

Gregersen, E. (2020). *Elon Musk*. https://www.britannica.com/biography/ Elon-Musk

Halsted, J. W. (2009). *Some of my best friends are books: Guiding gifted readers* (3rd ed.). Great Potential Press.

Hamayan, E. V., & Damico, J. S. (1991). Developing and using a second language. In E. V. Hamayan & J. S. Damico (Eds.), *Limiting bias in the assessment of bilingual students* (pp. 39–76). PRO-ED.

Hammond, Z. (2015). *Culturally responsive teaching and the brain: Promoting authentic engagement and rigor among culturally and linguistically diverse students*. Corwin.

Harris, B., Plucker, J. A., Rapp, K. E., & Martínez, R. S. (2009). Identifying gifted and talented English language learners: A case study. *Journal for the Education of the Gifted, 32*(3), 368–393. https://doi. org/10.4219/jeg-2009-858

Hildreth, G. H. (1966). *Introduction to the gifted*. McGraw-Hill.

History.com Editors. (2020). *Nikola Tesla*. https://www.history.com/top ics/inventions/nikola-tesla

Hoover, S. M., Sayler, M., & Feldhusen, J. F. (1993). Cluster grouping of gifted students at the elementary level. *Roeper Review, 16*(1), 13–15. https://doi.org/10.1080/02783199309553527

Hynes, A. M., & Hynes-Berry, M. (1986). *Bibliotherapy: The interactive process: A handbook*. Routledge.

Idang, G. E. (2015). African culture and values. *Phronimon, 16*(2), 97–111.

Ilhan for Congress. (n.d.). *Ilhan Omar's story*. https://ilhanomar.com/about

Iowa Department of Education. (2008). *Identifying gifted and talented English language learners: Grades K–12*. The Connie Belin and Jacqueline

N. Blank International Center for Gifted Education and Talent Development. https://educateiowa.gov/sites/files/ed/documents/Identify GiftedTalentedELL.pdf

Isaacson, W. (2007). *20 things you need to know about Einstein.* Time. http://content.time.com/time/specials/packages/article/0,28804, 1936731_1936743,00.html

Jiménez, R. T. (2017). Fostering the literacy development of Latino students. *Focus on Exceptional Children, 34*(6). https://doi.org/10.171 61/fec.v34i6.6789

Jones, R. (2017). *Chi Cheng Huang—saving Bolivia's street children.* Infinite Fire. http://infinitefire.org/info/chi-cheng-huang-saving-bolivias-st reet-children

Josephson, M. (2020). *Thomas Edison: American inventor.* Encyclopedia Britannica. https://www.britannica.com/biography/Thomas-Edison

Kaku, M. (n.d.). *Albert Einstein: German-American physicist.* https:// www.britannica.com/biography/Albert-Einstein

Khlystov, Y. (n.d.). *Personal space Chinese culture—is it any different?* https://www.laowaicareer.com/blog/chinese-personal-space-touch ing

Kitano, M. K., & Pedersen, K. S. (2002). Action research and practical inquiry teaching gifted English learners. *Journal for the Education of the Gifted, 26*(2), 132–147. https://doi.org/10.1177/016 235320202600204

LaCelle-Peterson, M. W., & Rivera, C. (1994). Is it real for all kids? A framework for equitable assessment policies for English language learners. *Harvard Educational Review, 64*(1), 55–75. https://doi.org/ 10.17763/haer.64.1.k3387733755817j7

Lambert, W. E., & Tucker, G. R. (1979). *Bilingual education of children: The St. Lambert experiment.* Newbury House.

Lau v. Nichols, 414 U.S. 563 (1974). https://www.oyez.org/cases/1973/ 72-6520

Leubering, J. E. (2020). *Chimamanda Ngozi Adichie: Nigerian author.* Encyclopedia Britannica. https://www.britannica.com/biography/Ch imamanda-Ngozi-Adichie

Long, C. (2015, April 23). How do we increase teacher quality in low-income schools? *NEA Today.*

Lonigan, C. J., & Shanahan, T. (2009). *Developing early literacy: Report of the national literacy panel: A scientific synthesis of early literacy development and implications for interventions* (ED508381). ERIC. https://files.eric.ed.gov/fulltext/ED508381.pdf

Marland, S. P., Jr. (1972). *Education of the gifted and talented: Report to the Congress of the United States by the U.S. Commissioner of Education and background papers submitted to the U.S. Office of Education,* 2 vols. U.S. Government Printing Office. (Government Documents, Y4.L 11/2: G36)

Marzano, R. J., Pickering, D., & Pollock, J. E. (2001). *Classroom instruction that works: Research-based strategies for increasing student achievement.* ASCD.

Matthews, D. J., & Foster, J. F. (2005). *Being smart about gifted children: A guidebook for parents and educators.* Great Potential Press.

Matthews, M. S., & Castellano, J. A. (Eds.). (2014). *Talent development for English language learners: Identifying and developing potential.* Prufrock Press.

McBee, M. T. (2006). A descriptive analysis of referral sources for gifted identification screening by race and socioeconomic status. *Journal of Secondary Gifted Education, 17*(2), 103–111. https://doi.org/10.4219/jsge-2006-686

McBee, M. T., Peters, S. J., & Waterman, C. (2013). Combining scores in multiple-criteria assessment systems. *Gifted Child Quarterly, 58*(1), 69–89. https://doi.org/10.1177/0016986213513794

McCormick, K., & Marshall, R. (n.d.). *Gifted education handbook: School District of Palm Beach County.* The School District of Palm Beach County. https://www.palmbeachschools.org/UserFiles/Servers/Server_270532/File/ESE/Gifted/Gifted-Handbook.pdf

McGowan, M. R., Runge, T. J., & Pedersen, J. A. (2016). Using curriculum-based measures for identifying gifted learners. *Roeper Review, 38*(2), 93–106. https://doi.org/10.1080/02783193.2016.1150376

Melton, A. P. (2005). Indigenous justice systems and tribal society. In W. D. McCaslin (Ed.), *Justice as healing: Indigenous ways. Writings on community peacemaking and restorative justice from the Native Law Centre* (pp. 108–120). Living Justice Press.

Mun, R. U., Langley, S. D., Ware, S., Gubbins, E. J., Siegle, D., Callahan, C. M., McCoach, D. B., Hamilton, R. (2016). *Effective practices for identifying and serving gifted English learners in gifted education: A systemic review of the literature.* National Center for Research on Gifted Education. https://ncrge.uconn.edu/wp-content/uploads/sites/982/2016/01/NCRGE_EL_Lit-Review.pdf

Musetti, B. (2009). *Don't question my authority: The power and pedagogy of English only: The transition of a bilingual school to "English only."* Lambert Academic Publishing.

National Association for Gifted Children. (n.d.). *Identification.* https://www.nagc.org/resources-publications/gifted-education-practices/identification

National Association for Gifted Children. (2010). *Redefining giftedness for a new century: Shifting the paradigm* [Position statement]. https://www.nagc.org/sites/default/files/Position%20Statement/Redefining%20Giftedness%20for%20a%20New%20Century.pdf

National Association for Gifted Children & Council of State Directors of Programs for the Gifted. (2015). *2014–2015 state of the states in gifted education: Policy and practice data.* https://www.nagc.org/sites/default/files/key%20reports/2014-2015%20State%20of%20the%20States%20%28final%29.pdf

National Center for Education Statistics. (2010). *Status and trends in the education of racial and ethnic groups.* https://nces.ed.gov/pubs2010/2010015.pdf

Nazario, S. (2006). *Enrique's journey: The story of a boy's dangerous odyssey to reunite with his mother.* Random House.

No Child Left Behind Act, 20 U.S.C. §6301 (2001). https://www.congress.gov/107/plaws/publ110/PLAW-107publ110.pdf

Parrett, W., & Budge, K. (2016). *How does poverty influence learning?* Edutopia. https://www.edutopia.org/blog/how-does-poverty-influence-learning-william-parrett-kathleen-budge

PBS. (n.d.). *Tesla's early years.* https://www.pbs.org/tesla/ll/ll_early.html

Peters, S. J. (2016). The bright versus gifted comparison. *Gifted Child Today, 39*(2), 125–127. https://doi.org/10.1177/1076217516628917

Pfeiffer, S., & Jarosewich, T. (2003). *Gifted rating scales.* Pearson.

Pierce, R. L., Adams, C. M., Speirs Neumeister, K. L., Cassady, J. C., Dixon, F. A., & Cross, T. L. (2006). Development of an identification procedure for a large urban school corporation: Identifying culturally diverse and academically gifted elementary students. *Roeper Review, 29*(2), 113–118.

Public Schools of North Carolina. (n.d.). *Child count.* https://ec.ncpub licschools.gov/reports-data/child-count

Radin, P. (2015). *African folktales.* Princeton University Press.

Raphael, T. E. (1982). Question-answering strategies for children. *The Reading Teacher, 36*(2), 186–190.

Rasberry, C. N., Slade, S., Lohrmann, D. K., & Valois, R. F. (2015). Lessons learned from the whole child and coordinated school health approaches. *Journal of School Health, 85*(11), 759–765. https://doi. org/10.1111/josh.12307

Rea, C. (2015, October). *GATE identification FAQ's.* San Diego Unified School District. https://www.sandiegounified.org/UserFiles/Servers/ Server_27732394/File/Departments/Gifted%20and%20Talented %20Education%20(GATE)/GATE%20Assessment/GATE%20Id entification%20FAQ%27s%20%2010%202015-Carrie%20Rea _0.pdf

Renzulli, J. S. (2005). The three-ring conception of giftedness: A developmental model for promoting creative productivity. In R. J. Sternberg & J. E. Davidson (Eds.), *Conceptions of giftedness* (2nd ed., pp. 246– 279). https://doi.org/10.1017/cbo9780511610455.015

Resnick, D., & Goodman, M. (1997). *Northwest education.* Northwest Educational Laboratory Resources.

Robisheaux, J., & Banbury, M. M. (2002). Voice and validation: Creativity and bilingualism. In J. A. Castellano & E. Diaz (Eds.), *Reaching new horizons: Gifted and talented education for culturally and linguistically diverse students* (pp. 76–93). Allyn & Bacon.

Ross, P. O. (1993). *National excellence: A case for developing America's talent.* U.S. Department of Education, Office of Educational Research and Improvement.

Runge, T., & McGowan, M. (2012, September). Identification of giftedness in Pennsylvania. *Pennsylvania Psychologist.*

Saccuzzo, D. P., & Johnson, N. E. (1995). Traditional psychometric tests and proportionate representation: An intervention and program evaluation study. *Psychological Assessment, 7*(2), 183–194. https://doi.org/10.1037/1040-3590.7.2.183

Sanchez, C. (2017). *English language learners: How your state is doing.* NPR. https://www.npr.org/sections/ed/2017/02/23/512451228/5-million-english-language-learners-a-vast-pool-of-talent-at-risk

Shrodes, C. (1949). *Bibliotherapy: A theoretical and clinical-experimental study* [Unpublished doctoral dissertation]. University of California, Berkeley.

Sparks, S. D., & Harwin, A. (2017). *Too few ELL students land in gifted classes.* Education Week. https://www.edweek.org/ew/articles/2017/06/21/too-few-ell-students-land-in-gifted.html

Stambaugh, T., & Chandler, K. L. (2012). *Effective curriculum for underserved gifted students.* Prufrock Press.

Stambaugh, T., & VanTassel-Baska, J. (2018). *Jacob's Ladder Reading Comprehension Program: Grades 1–2* (2nd ed.). Prufrock Press.

Stepien, W. J., & Pyke, S. L. (1997). Designing problem-based learning units. *Journal for the Education of the Gifted, 20*(4), 380–400. https://doi.org/10.1177/016235329702000404

Sullivan, P., & Lilburn, P. (2002). *Good questions for math teaching: Why ask them and what to ask, K–6.* Math Solutions.

Szabos, J. (1989). Bright child, gifted learner. *Challenge, 34.*

Tomlinson, C. A. (2014). *The differentiated classroom: Responding to the needs of all learners* (2nd ed.). ASCD.

University of Massachusetts Medical School. (2013). *Katherine Luzuriaga named one of TIME magazine's TIME 100.* https://www.umassmed.edu/news/news-archives/2013/04/luzuriaga-named-time-100

U.S. Census Bureau. (2017). *Facts for features: Hispanic heritage month 2017.* https://www.census.gov/newsroom/facts-for-features/2017/hispanic-heritage.html

U.S. Department of Education. (n.d.). *Our nation's English learners: What are their characteristics?* https://www2.ed.gov/datastory/el-characteristics/index.html

U.S. National Library of Medicine. (2015). *Dr. Helen Rodriguez-Trias.* https://cfmedicine.nlm.nih.gov/physicians/biography_273.html

VanTassel-Baska, J., & Stambaugh, T. (2016). *Jacob's Ladder Reading Comprehension Program: Nonfiction grade 5*. Prufrock Press.

Virginia Department of Education. (2017). *2016–2017 gifted annual report for all divisions*. https:www.doe.virginia.gov/statistics_reports/gifted/membership/2017-gifted.pdf

Vygotsky, L. (2012). *Thought and language* (E. Hanfmann, G. Vakar, & A. Kozulin, Trans.; Rev. ed.). MIT Press.

Wang, Q. (2009). Are Asians forgetful? Perception, retention, and recall in episodic remembering. *Cognition, 111*(1), 123–131. https://doi.org/10.1016/j.cognition.2009.01.004

Webb, J. T., Gore, J. L., Amend, E. R., & DeVries, A. R. (2007). *A parent's guide to gifted children*. Great Potential Press.

WIDA. (n.d.). *WIDA consortium*. https://wida.wisc.edu/memberships/consortium

Appendix A
Implementing a Yearlong Book Study

Identifying and Supporting Gifted English Language Learners may be used as a yearlong book study for ELL teachers, AIG teachers, classroom teachers, and administrators. The following sections include a book study introduction that might be shared with participants, as well as a suggested timeline and description of actions for key players throughout the year.

Book Study Introduction

Identifying and supporting gifted English language learners (ELLs) is a relatively new concept, with the majority of literature on the topic having taken place in the past 2 decades. Research shows that there is a large disparity between ELLs identified as gifted in comparison with native English speakers identified as gifted. Accordingly, only 2% of identified gifted learners are dually identified as English learning, while research indicates that at least 10% or more of the population holds academic or intellectual abilities far above those of their peers. So why aren't more ELLs identified as gifted?

Identifying and Supporting Gifted English Language Learners explores the current research in the field and presents a practical guide for identifying and supporting gifted learners within schools, districts, and states. This guide is based on best practices gained from previous research studies in conjunction with firsthand teaching experience in the field by the author. The purpose of this book is to inspire action by key players in this work, including ELL and academically or intellectually gifted (AIG) teachers, classroom teachers, school administrators, district/state leaders, parents, families, and the greater community, to identify more gifted ELLs. It presents guidance for each key player in how to carry out their role to be most effective in casting a wider net to increase the number of identified gifted ELLs.

Suggested Timeline

- ▶ **August/September**—Introduction: Who Are Gifted English Language Learners?
- ▶ **September/October**—Chapter 1: Support: Setting a Foundation to Support Gifted ELLs
- ▶ **November**—Chapter 2: Plan: Creating a Plan for Teaching Gifted ELLs
- ▶ **December**—Chapter 3: Listen: How to Listen and Observe for Potentially Gifted ELLs
- ▶ **January/February**—Chapter 4: Act: Putting Action Behind Ideas and Research to Identify Gifted ELLs
- ▶ **March**—Chapter 5: Teach: How to Teach Identified Gifted ELLs
- ▶ **April**—Conclusion: The Ongoing Process of Identifying and Supporting Gifted ELLs

In addition, actions that can be taken by each key player throughout the year are outlined on the following page.

When	Who	What
August/September	ELL, AIG, and classroom teachers	Collaborate to discuss current and potential students.
	ELL and AIG teachers	Host parent outreach event.
October–December	ELL, AIG, and classroom teachers	Pulse check-ins and team planning.
January/February	ELL and AIG teachers	Host parent outreach event.
March/April	ELL, AIG, and classroom teachers	Ongoing planning and student data collection for potentially gifted ELLs.
May	ELL, AIG, and classroom teachers; administrators	Reflection of the year (e.g., What went well? Where can we continue to improve?).
Summer	ELL, AIG, and classroom teachers; administrators	Long-range planning and considering program adoptions/modifications.

Appendix B
Resources for Building Relationships

This section provides resources to guide you through the processes discussed in specific chapters. These resources are intended to support AIG, ELL, and classroom teachers to build relationships with students and colleagues.

- ▸ Setting the Stage for Effective AIG and ELL Collaboration
- ▸ The "Great Exchange" Meeting

In addition, the following relationship-building resources mentioned throughout the book may be accessed at https://www.prufrock.com/Identifying-and-Supporting-Gifted-English-Language-Learners-Resources.aspx.

- ▸ Gingerbread Activity: Getting to Know You and Your Culture
- ▸ Student Learning Interest Survey
- ▸ Rubric to Guide Student Reflection

Setting the Stage for Effective AIG and ELL Collaboration

AIG Teacher Name: _____

Room # or Location: _____

Email Address: _____

Phone #: _____

Schedule: _____

When is your planning period? _____

When is your lunchtime? _____

When is your "busy" time of year usually? _____

What are some BIG pieces of your job, and when do they usually take

place? _____

_____

How many certified and/or catalyst students do you have? _____

ELL Teacher Name: _____

Room # or Location: _____

Email Address: _____

Phone #: _____

Schedule: _____

When is your planning period? _____

When is your lunchtime? _____

When is your "busy" time of year usually? _____

What are some BIG pieces of your job, and when do they usually take place? _____

_____

How many certified and/or catalyst students do you have? _____

How many direct ELLs do you have on your caseload? _____

Is there anything about you that you would like for me to know?

_____

_____

_____

Setting Up an Effective Planning Questionnaire

▶ How would you like for us to plan? (circle one):

Together   Independently and then share/discuss

▶ When would be best for us to plan together? (circle one):

Before school   Afterschool   Lunch/planning time

▶ How often would you like to plan? (circle one; at least once a quarter is suggested):

Once/quarter   Once/month   Once/week   Every other day

▶ When is your busiest time of year?

_____

▶ When is a set time when we could meet? (e.g., first Thursday of each month)

_____

The "Great Exchange" Meeting

Getting Started (10 minutes)

The ELL and AIG teachers should explain their answers to the following questions:

- What is your role?
- What does your role entail or look like on a regular basis?

Recording Key Details (5–10 minutes)

The ELL and AIG teachers should review the key details they will need to share in the following table and fill in their answer to their questions. By filling in your section beforehand, each teacher has the necessary think time so they will be better prepared to share for the next section.

Key Details for ELL Teacher to Share	Key Details for AIG Teacher to Share
<ul><li>How do you identify English language learners?</li><li>What is the process for exiting?</li><li>How do you support ELLs?</li><li>What are some ways to differentiate for high-achieving ELLs who may be gifted?</li></ul>	<ul><li>How do you identify gifted learners?</li><li>What does this process look like or consist of?</li><li>What are some ways that an ELL teacher could nurture giftedness?</li><li>What would be some indicators that an ELL may be gifted?</li></ul>

ELL Teacher's Important Shared Details	AIG Teacher's Important Shared Details

Sharing (10–20 minutes)

The ELL and AIG teachers should take turns answering each of the questions within their key details box to provide pertinent information to the other.

Reflecting (5 minutes)

The ELL and AIG teachers should reflect on any areas that they would like to learn more about and consider sharing any relevant resources that may help the other to advocate, identify, or support gifted ELLs.

Appendix C
Resources to Extend Students' Thinking

The resources included in this appendix offer lessons and activities to support students to think critically and engage in higher order thinking activities. These activities also support students' socioemotional needs:

- Bibliotherapy Sample Unit
- Growth Mindset Lesson: Change Your Words, Change Your Outlook

Additionally, the following activity pages may be accessed at https://www.prufrock.com/Identifying-and-Supporting-Gifted-English-Language-Learners-Resources.aspx.

- Team-Building Task Cards: Let's Get Together Yeah, Yeah, Yeah (With a Hint of Figurative Language)
- Question-Answer Relationships Sort Activity

Bibliotherapy Sample Unit

Unit Objective: Students will create a photo journal or photo essay using Adobe Spark to tell their story (i.e., their cultural story, what makes them different, or their personal journey).

Integrated Standards/Ideas: Main idea with supporting details, theme, character traits, immigration, geography, culture, language.

Photo Journal Rubric:

	1	2	3	4
Includes a catchy title	No title	Includes a plain title	Includes a fun title	Includes an eye-catching and fun title
Has at least five meaningful photos/ pictures	Has only two pictures	Has three photos or pictures	Has four or five photos, but they are not meaningful	Has five meaningful photos
Tells a story/ explains their journey/ explains what makes them different	Does not tell a story or have a message	Tells part of a story but has no clear message	Includes two parts of a story (beginning, middle, end) or has a clear message	Includes all parts of a story and has a clear message/ explanation of what makes them different
Includes at least one video interview or one voice recording	No video or voice recording	Limited video or unclear voice recording	Has either a video or voice recording	Has a video or voice recording that supports their story/ message
Created for a specific audience	No specific audience	Some thought or effort put into target audience	Target audience is clear but needs some support	Target audience is clear and well developed

Lesson 1: Launch: What Is Different?

▶ Building Background: Divide the class into two equal groups to play a game of charades. Students will act out the phrase on their card and then have their team guess the phrase. The silent charade cards are:

I need to go to the bathroom.	I am hungry. What time is lunch?	What time is recess?
Can I borrow a pencil?	My name is. . . . What is your name?	Where is the office?

▶ Read Aloud, Think Aloud: Explain that the game of charades relates to today's text, the book *No English* by Jacqueline Jules and Amy Huntington. The story follows a new student named Blanca from Argentina who tries to fit in with her second-grade classmates. Tell students, "I wonder if she wanted to say any phrases like the ones in our game and how her classmates reacted to her? Let's find out as we read." During the read aloud, pause to share your thinking about what is happening in the book (e.g., "I wonder why Blanca is drawing pictures instead of doing classwork," or "Diane doesn't seem to be very nice toward Blanca for drawing. I think this would make Blanca feel badly.")

▶ Guide students to engage in a discussion about the text. All students should have a chance to voice their thoughts. Have students turn and talk to their partner while you walk around to listen to students' responses. Make eye contact with students or tap students on the shoulder who had notable responses to inquire if they can share their response. This strategy shows students that their voice is heard but also takes pressure off of students who may be more shy. For the discussion, pose one question at a time, listen to partners, let certain students share, and then move on to the next question. Guiding questions include:

▹ Why do you think drawing pictures helps Blanca? Can you think of a time when you were scared or embarrassed because you felt different? What did you do?

▹ Diana starts to notice that Blanca is afraid and wants to help. How does Diana try to help Blanca?

▹ Have you ever had a time when you saw that someone was scared? How did you help them?

▹ What does Mrs. Bertram help the class to understand? Do you think this is an important lesson? Why?

▶ After the discussion, ask students to think about what can make each person different, using at least 30 seconds or more of think time. Students will then share their response with their same turn-and-talk partner. Afterward they will write their response on a sticky note.

▶ Next, create an anchor chart with student input about things that can make each person different (not strange or weird). This can include language, food, family, looks, feelings about others, and what is important in their lives (e.g., college, family business, supporting loved ones, etc.).

▶ Finally, students will complete an exit ticket: *Write, draw, or act out a "You're Special" note to someone and explain what you like about them that makes them special.*

Lesson 2: How Can Feeling Different Feel?

▶ Review the "What Is Different?" anchor chart from Lesson 1.

▶ Read aloud *One Green Apple* by Eve Bunting, a book about a girl named Farah who is starting at a new school where no one speaks her language. She feels alone because all she can do is listen and nod. One day, on a field trip at an apple orchard, Farah learns that there are many similarities between her old life and her new life. As she is learning about making apple cider, she starts to feel connected to her new surroundings and classmates.

▸ Help students draw a connection between this text and the previous text, *No English*.

▸ Have students work in small groups or with a partner to read the graphic novel *The Arrival* by Shaun Tan. Students will write 2–3 sentences to explain the gist of the text on a sticky note and attach it to a class anchor chart.

▸ Exit Ticket: Students will turn and tell their partner their response to this question: *Why did I have you read this text, and how does it relate to the idea that different is different, but not bad?*

Lesson 3: What Makes You Different?

▸ Have students review *The Arrival* and then, on a sticky note, write what makes them different.

▸ Introduce a photo journal using a YouTube video (conduct a search for kid-friendly videos) and discuss what elements a good photo journal will include.

▸ Draw a connection between *The Arrival* and a photo journal or story (e.g., "Pictures from the text *The Arrival* are like a photo journal because they show what life was like for that character at different places in his journey.").

▸ Students will turn and talk to think about what their photo journal could include, then write down three ideas they have for their photo journal that will explain what makes them different.

▸ Read aloud the book *Dear Juno* by Soyung Pak. The text is about a boy named Juno and his Korean grandmother exchanging letters. The grandmother writes in Korean and includes photos, while Juno creates drawings. They are able to communicate in their own way even though they cannot read or write the same language. Juno and his grandmother exchange letters in their own way that tells Juno's grandmother to come for a visit. The grandmother replies with a picture of an airplane. It is a heartwarming story about the power of symbols and connection in communication.

▶ After the read aloud, students will turn and talk to discuss: *How did Juno and his grandmother create a photo journal? Who would be your audience for your photo journal? Why?*

Lesson 4: What Is a Photo Journal?

▶ Students will recap "What is a photo journal?" with their partner and share their idea for their photo journal. Partners must give two pieces of feedback about their partner's photo journal ideas—one positive comment and one suggestion.

▶ Introduce and explain the photo journal rubric.

▶ Students will draw a rough draft of their photo journal for approval that must include their story/message and target audience. Once approved, students may start making their photo journal using Adobe Spark.

▶ After checking rough drafts, read aloud *The Colour of Home* by Mary Hoffman. The book is about a first grader named Hassan from Somalia. Hassan misses his home country, but with the help of his parents and teacher, he is able to create a project to remember home. By creating this project, Hassan is able to understand and cope with his various feelings about fleeing a war-torn country.

▶ Ask questions about the text to support students to understand their own feelings: *When was a time when you were homesick? What did you do to feel better? What would you make to help you remember home?*

▶ Exit ticket: *What is your story?*

Lesson 5: What Is Your Story?

▶ Have students tell a new partner about their story and their target audience. Partners must give two pieces of feedback about their partner's photo journal ideas—one positive comment and one suggestion.

▶ Review the photo journal rubric.

▶ Students will continue working on their photo journal using Adobe Spark. Provide technology support or photo feedback as necessary.

▶ Students should continue working as they watch/hear a reading of *The Name Jar* by Yangsook Choi on YouTube.

Lesson 6: Photo Journal Presentations

▶ Review the project and its purpose by revisiting the original "What Is Different?" anchor chart about what makes everyone unique (see Lesson 1).

▶ Students will take turns presenting their Adobe Spark photo journal to the class while classmates listen to provide feedback using the provided rubric.

▶ Recap and emphasize the importance of being different and that being different is not strange or weird.

Growth Mindset Lesson: Change Your Words, Change Your Outlook

Lesson Objective: Students will be able to understand the difference between a fixed mindset and a growth mindset, using the book *Your Fantastic Elastic Brain: Stretch It, Shape It* by JoAnn Deak.

Essential Question: What type of mindset do you have when you face challenges or roadblocks?

Lesson Overview:

- ▶ 5–10 minutes: Student Self-Reflection Survey (to be completed independently)
- ▶ 10–20 minutes: Read aloud, think aloud using *Your Fantastic Elastic Brain*
- ▶ 5 minutes: Turn and talk with partner, lesson recap
- ▶ 15 minutes: Student choice of growth mindset activity
- ▶ 10 minutes: Whole-group share

Student Self-Reflection Survey

	True	False
1. I am not good at some things.		
2. It is okay to fail because I can learn from it.		
3. I don't like it when others do better than me.		
4. I like trying new things even I am not good at them yet.		
5. I feel good when I am better at something than others.		
6. I feel good when others are good at something, too.		
7. I like it when I can do something that others cannot.		
8. How intelligent I am can change.		
9. I think people are either born intelligent or unintelligent. You can't change that.		
10. I like to be challenged because it means that I am growing.		

Answer: The odd numbers are fixed mindset thoughts, and the even numbers are growth mindset thoughts.

Read Aloud, Think Aloud

- ▶ Introduce the text *Your Fantastic Elastic Brain.* Explain that today, the class is going to read aloud a text about all of the amazing things that the brain does and helps people to do.
- ▶ Read the text aloud while pausing to share what you are thinking about the information that you are learning as you read (e.g., "Wow, I didn't know that the hippocampus. . . .").
- ▶ Draw students' attention back to the page in the book about learning how to play soccer. Reread that page. Share a story about a time when you tried something new that was hard or you failed at something in the beginning. Ask students to think about something that they tried but were not very good at when they first tried it.

Turn and Talk

- ▶ Students should turn and tell their partner about a time when they struggled to learn something new and what they did to get better at it.
- ▶ Next, ask students to think about a time when their brain had to grow because they made a mistake. Have students turn and tell their partner about a time when they failed and how they learned from that failure to help their brain grow.
- ▶ Recap the importance of making mistakes in order to stretch the brain.

Student Choice of Growth Mindset Activity

Present the following different choices of activities to students. Students may work independently, with a partner, or small group to complete the activity of their choice.

Draw Your Fixed Mindset and Name It	Create a Self-Talk Journal	Create a Turn-Around Phrase Book
Create a drawing of your fixed mindset. Think about what it would look like and why. What nickname would you give it, and why? Make sure to add lots of details that make your drawing special to you. Some examples may include drawings of times when you had a fixed mindset, like when you had to learn how to ride a bicycle and gave up too quickly.	Write down a conversation of self-talk that you have had or could have when you get frustrated. Self-talk is the voice inside your head that tells you what you are thinking. Some examples of self-talk include, "Wow, I look great in this shirt," or "This is too hard—I can't do this!" Record your thinking in a situation when you have been frustrated. Make sure to include how you felt and why.	Create a table that includes fixed mindset phrases on one side and then how to change those phrases into a growth mindset phrases on the other side. An example could be: "This is too hard; I can't do this!" (fixed mindset) and "This is hard, but if I practice at it, it will become easier" (growth mindset). Try to come up with as many phrases as you can.

Choose an Accountability Partner and Create a Go-to Plan of Support	Create a Mindset Skit	Make a Poster for the Class
After you choose your accountability partner, write down your plan to help each other when one of you gets frustrated and needs a growth mindset pep talk. Write down some phrases that you can tell your partner to help them find a growth mindset.	Create a skit or play of a situation where one or more persons needs help finding a growth mindset. The person may have a fixed mindset or just need a growth mindset pep talk. Write down what each person in the skit will say, and then practice as a group reading your lines in order.	Create an anchor chart for the class to teach the difference between a growth mindset and a fixed mindset. Make sure to include a heading for your poster, a description of the difference between a fixed and growth mindset, and at least one picture.

Whole-Class Share

▶ Students will share their choice of growth mindset activity with the class.

▶ Reinforce the importance of a growth mindset and display any posters or art to encourage positive reinforcement when students begin to struggle.

About the Author

Mary C. Campbell is an award-winning and Nationally Board Certified English as a new/second language teacher from Charlotte, NC. She is currently pursuing her Ph.D. in curriculum studies and instruction at Florida State University.